Let's Keep in Touch

Follow Us Online

Visit US at

www.EffortlessMath.com

 https://www.facebook.com/Effortlessmath

 https://goo.gl/2B6qWW

Online Math Lessons

It's easy! Here's how it works.

1- Request a FREE introductory session.

2- Meet a Math tutor online.

3- Start Learning Math in Minutes.

Send Email to: info@EffortlessMath.com

www.EffortlessMath.com

... So Much More Online!

- ✓ FREE Math lessons

- ✓ More Math learning books!

- ✓ Mathematics Worksheets

- ✓ Online Math Tutors

Need a PDF version of this book?

Send email to: info@EffortlessMath.com

PSSA Mathematics Workbook For Grade 6

Step-By-Step Guide to Preparing for the PSSA Math Test 2019

By

Reza Nazari

& Ava Ross

Copyright © 2018

Reza Nazari & Ava Ross

All rights reserved. No part of this publication may be reproduced, stored in a retrieval system, or transmitted in any form or by any means, electronic, mechanical, photocopying, recording, scanning, or otherwise, except as permitted under Section 107 or 108 of the 1976 United States Copyright Ac, without permission of the author.

All inquiries should be addressed to:

info@effortlessMath.com

www.EffortlessMath.com

ISBN-13: 978-1725876200

ISBN-10: 1725876205

Published by: Effortless Math Education

www.EffortlessMath.com

Description

The goal of this book is simple. It will help your student incorporates the best method and the right strategies to prepare for the PSSA Mathematics test FAST and EFFECTIVELY.

PSSA Mathematics Workbook is full of specific and detailed material that will be key to succeeding on the PSSA Math. It's filled with the critical math concepts a student will need in order to ace the test. Math concepts in this book break down the topics, so the material can be quickly grasped. Examples are worked step-by-step, so you learn exactly what to do.

PSSA Mathematics Workbook helps your student to focus on all Math topics that students will need to ace the PSSA Math test. This book with 2 complete PSSA tests is all your student will ever need to fully prepare for the PSSA Math.

This workbook includes practice test questions. It contains easy-to-read essential summaries that highlight the key areas of the PSSA Math test. Effortless Math test study guide reviews the most important components of the PSSA Math test. Anyone planning to take the PSSA Math test should take advantage of the review material and practice test questions contained in this study guide.

Inside the pages of this workbook, students can learn basic math operations in a structured manner with a complete study program to help them understand essential math skills. It also has many exciting features, including:

- Dynamic design and easy-to-follow activities
- A fun, interactive and concrete learning process
- Targeted, skill-building practices
- Math topics are grouped by category, so students can focus on the topics they struggle on
- All solutions for the exercises are included, so you will always find the answers
- 2 Complete PSSA Math Practice Tests that reflect the format and question types on PSSA

PSSA Mathematics Workbook is a breakthrough in Math learning — offering a winning formula and the most powerful methods for learning basic Math topics confidently. Each section offers step-by-step instruction and helpful hints, with a few topics being tackled each chapter. Two complete REAL PSSA Math tests are provided at the back of the book to refine your student's Math skills.

***PSSA Mathematics Workbook* is the only book your student will ever need to master Basic Math topics!** It can be used as a self-study course – you do not need to work with a Math tutor. (It can also be used with a Math tutor).

Ideal for self-study as well as for classroom usage.

About the Author

Reza Nazari is the author of more than 100 Math learning books including:
– **Math and Critical Thinking Challenges:** For the Middle and High School Student
– **GRE Math in 30 Days**
– **ASVAB Math Workbook 2018 – 2019**
– **Effortless Math Education Workbooks**
– and many more Mathematics books …

Reza is also an experienced Math instructor and a test–prep expert who has been tutoring students since 2008. Reza is the founder of Effortless Math Education, a tutoring company that has helped many students raise their standardized test scores—and attend the colleges of their dreams. Reza provides an individualized custom learning plan and the personalized attention that makes a difference in how students view math.

You can contact Reza via email at:
reza@EffortlessMath.com

Find Reza's professional profile at:
goo.gl/zoC9rJ

Contents

Chapter 1: Whole Number Operations 11
    Adding Whole Numbers 12
    Subtracting Whole Numbers 13
    Dividing Whole Numbers 14
    Multiplying Whole Numbers 15
    Rounding Whole Numbers 16
    Whole Number Estimation 17
    Answers of Worksheets – Chapter 1 19

Chapter 2: Arithmetic and Number Theory 22
    Simplifying Fractions 23
    Adding and Subtracting Fractions 24
    Multiplying and Dividing Fractions 25
    Adding Mixed Numbers 26
    Subtract Mixed Numbers 27
    Multiplying Mixed Numbers 28
    Dividing Mixed Numbers 29
    Comparing Decimals 30
    Rounding Decimals 31
    Adding and Subtracting Decimals 32
    Multiplying and Dividing Decimals 33
    Converting Between Fractions, Decimals and Mixed Numbers 34
    Factoring Numbers 35
    Greatest Common Factor 36
    Least Common Multiple 37
    Divisibility Rules 38
    Test Preparation 39
    Answers of Worksheets – Chapter 2 44

Chapter 3: Real Numbers and Integers 52
    Adding and Subtracting Integers 53
    Multiplying and Dividing Integers 54
    Ordering Integers and Numbers 55

Arrange, Order, and Comparing Integers 56
Order of Operations 57
Mixed Integer Computations 58
Absolute Value 59
Integers and Absolute Value 60
Classifying Real Numbers Venn Diagram 61
Test Preparation 63
Answers of Worksheets – Chapter 3 64

Chapter 4: Percent 68

Percentage Calculations 69
Converting Between Percent, Fractions, and Decimals 70
Percent Problems 71
Find What Percentage a Number Is of Another 72
Find a Percentage of a Given Number 73
Percent of Increase and Decrease 74
Test Preparation 76
Answers of Worksheets – Chapter 4 81

Chapter 5: Algebraic Expressions 88

Expressions and Variables 89
Simplifying Variable Expressions 90
Translate Phrases into an Algebraic Statement 91
The Distributive Property 92
Evaluating One Variable 93
Evaluating Two Variables 94
Combining like Terms 95
Test Preparation 96
Answers of Worksheets – Chapter 5 97

Chapter 6: Equations 100

One–Step Equations 101
One–Step Equation Word Problems 102
Two–Step Equations 103
Two–Step Equation Word Problems 104

Multi–Step Equations 105
Test Preparation 106
Answers of Worksheets – Chapter 6 110

Chapter 7: Proportions and Ratios 115
Writing Ratios 116
Proportional Ratios 117
Simplifying Ratios 118
Create a Proportion 119
Similar Figures 120
Similar Figure Word Problems 121
Ratio and Rates Word Problems 122
Test Preparation 123
Answers of Worksheets – Chapter 7 125

Chapter 8: Inequalities 129
Graphing Single–Variable Inequalities 130
One–Step Inequalities 131
Two–Step Inequalities 132
Multi–Step Inequalities 133
Test Preparation 134
Answers of Worksheets – Chapter 8 136

Chapter 9: Exponents and Radicals 139
Multiplication Property of Exponents 140
Division Property of Exponents 141
Powers of Products and Quotients 142
Zero and Negative Exponents 143
Negative Exponents and Negative Bases 144
Writing Scientific Notation 145
Square Roots 146
Test Preparation 147
Answers of Worksheets – Chapter 9 149

Chapter 10: Measurements 153
Inches and Centimeters 154

Metric Units 155

Distance Measurement 156

Weight Measurement 157

Test Preparation 158

Answers of Worksheets – Chapter 10 159

Chapter 11: Plane Figures 162

The Pythagorean Theorem 163

Area of Triangles 164

Perimeter of Polygons 165

Area and Circumference of Circles 166

Area of Squares, Rectangles, and Parallelograms 167

Area of Trapezoids 168

Test Preparation 169

Answers of Worksheets – Chapter 11 172

Chapter 12: Solid Figures 175

Volume of Cubes 176

Volume of Rectangle Prisms 177

Surface Area of Cubes 178

Surface Area of a Rectangle Prism 179

Volume of a Cylinder 180

Surface Area of a Cylinder 181

Test Preparation 182

Answers of Worksheets – Chapter 12 184

Chapter 13: Statistics 186

Mean, Median, Mode, and Range of the Given Data 187

First Quartile, Second Quartile and Third Quartile of the Given Data 188

Box and Whisker Plots 189

Bar Graph 190

Stem–And–Leaf Plot 191

The Pie Graph or Circle Graph 192

Scatter Plots 193

Probability of Simple Events 194

Test Preparation 196

Answers of Worksheets – Chapter 13 201

PSSA Mathematics Practice Tests 210

PSSA Practice Test 1 212

PSSA Practice Test 2 224

PSSA Math Practice Tests Answers and Explanations 235

Chapter 1: Whole Number Operations

Topics that you'll learn in this chapter:

- ✓ Adding Whole Numbers
- ✓ Subtracting Whole Numbers
- ✓ Dividing Whole Numbers
- ✓ Multiplying Whole Numbers
- ✓ Rounding Whole Numbers
- ✓ Whole Number Estimation

Adding Whole Numbers

Helpful Hints

1– Line up the numbers.

2– Start with the unit place. (ones place)

3– Regroup if necessary.

4– Add the tens place.

5– Continue with other digits.

Example:

$$\begin{array}{r} 1,349 \\ +2,411 \\ \hline 3,760 \end{array}$$

✎ Add.

1) $\begin{array}{r} 1,158 \\ +\ 6,687 \\ \hline \end{array}$

2) $\begin{array}{r} 5,188 \\ +\ 1,298 \\ \hline \end{array}$

3) $\begin{array}{r} 5,756 \\ +\ 2,712 \\ \hline \end{array}$

4) $\begin{array}{r} 3,239 \\ +2,562 \\ \hline \end{array}$

5) $\begin{array}{r} 4,257 \\ +5,194 \\ \hline \end{array}$

6) $\begin{array}{r} 6,215 \\ +2,189 \\ \hline \end{array}$

✎ Find the missing numbers.

7) 1145 + ___ = 1276

8) 500 + 1000 = ___

9) 3200 + ___ = 4300

10) 455 + ___ = 1755

11) ___ + 720 = 1250

12) ___ + 670 = 2230

13) David sells gems. He finds a diamond in Istanbul and buys it for $3,433. Then, he flies to Cairo and purchases a bigger diamond for the bargain price of $5,922. How much does David spend on the two diamonds? _____

Subtracting Whole Numbers

Helpful Hints

1– Line up the numbers.

2– Start with the units place. (ones place)

3– Regroup if necessary.

4– Subtract the tens place.

5– Continue with other digits.

Example:

$$\begin{array}{r} 5,397 \\ -2,416 \\ \hline 2,981 \end{array}$$

✎ Subtract.

1) $\begin{array}{r} 8,519 \\ -5,422 \\ \hline \end{array}$

2) $\begin{array}{r} 6,222 \\ -4,331 \\ \hline \end{array}$

3) $\begin{array}{r} 7,821 \\ -3,212 \\ \hline \end{array}$

4) $\begin{array}{r} 8,756 \\ -6,712 \\ \hline \end{array}$

5) $\begin{array}{r} 9,290 \\ -3,829 \\ \hline \end{array}$

6) $\begin{array}{r} 5,117 \\ -4,216 \\ \hline \end{array}$

✎ Find the missing number.

7) 2223 – ___ = 1120

8) 3574 – ___ = 2245

9) 1124 – 578 = ___

10) 2300 – ___ = 1250

11) 3780 – 1890 = ___

12) 2880 – 2560 = ___

13) Jackson had $3,963 invested in the stock market until he lost $2,171 on those investments. How much money does he have in the stock market now?

Dividing Whole Numbers

Helpful Hints

– A typical division problem:

Dividend ÷ Divisor = Quotient

Example:

18,000 ÷ 90 = 200

– In division, we want to find how many times a number (divisor) is contained in another number (dividend).

– The result in a division problem is the quotient.

✍ Find answers.

1) 500 ÷ 100

2) 4000 ÷ 400

3) 1,500 ÷ 500

4) 1,800 ÷ 300

5) 2,700 ÷ 900

6) 800 ÷ 200

7) 1,400 ÷ 200

8) 2,500 ÷ 500

9) 4,800 ÷ 600

10) 9000 ÷ 200

11) 3,600 ÷ 600

12) 3,000 ÷ 500

13) 1000 ÷ 200

14) 4,500 ÷ 900

15) 1,200 ÷ 600

16) 6,000 ÷ 200

17) 9,000 ÷ 300

18) 2,800 ÷ 400

Multiplying Whole Numbers

Helpful Hints

– Learn the times tables first!

– For multiplication, line up the numbers you are multiplying.

– Start with the ones place.

– Continue with other digits

Example:

200 × 90 = 18,000

✎ Find the answers.

1) 2400 × 13

2) 1200 × 10

3) 3120 × 9

4) 4000 × 4

5) 2500 × 5

6) 3200 × 25

7) 4178 × 34

8) 9256 × 26

9) 3191 × 78

10) 4200 × 12

11) 6800 × 10

12) 8000 × 55

Rounding Whole Numbers

> *Helpful Hints*
>
> — Rounding is putting a number up or down to the nearest whole number or the nearest hundred, etc.
>
> **Example:**
>
> 64 rounded to the nearest ten is 60, because 64 is closer to 60 than to 70.

✎ Round each number to the underlined place value.

1) 1<u>9</u>72
   2000

2) 2,<u>9</u>95
   3000

3) 33<u>6</u>4
   3360

4) 12<u>8</u>1
   1280

5) 23<u>5</u>5

6) 13<u>3</u>4
   1330

7) 1,<u>2</u>03
   1,200

8) 14<u>5</u>7
   1460

9) 7<u>4</u>84
   7500

10) 19<u>1</u>4
    1910

11) 42<u>3</u>9
    4240

12) <u>9</u>,123
    9,000

13) 3,4<u>5</u>2
    3450

14) 2<u>5</u>69
    2700

15) 1,<u>2</u>30
    1,200

16) 7<u>6</u>98
    7700

17) 92<u>9</u>3
    9290

18) 52<u>3</u>7
    5230

19) 24<u>9</u>3
    2490

20) 2,<u>9</u>23
    3000

21) <u>9</u>,845
    10,000

22) 45<u>5</u>5

23) 6<u>9</u>39
    6900

24) 98<u>6</u>9
    9870

Whole Number Estimation

> **Helpful Hints**
>
> – To estimate means to make a rough guess or calculation.
>
> – To round means to simplify a number by scaling it slightly up or down.
>
> Example:
>
> 73 + 69 ≈ 140

✎ *Estimate the sum by rounding each added to the nearest ten.*

1) 582 + 277

2) 2771 + 1651

3) 7436 + 3575

4) 1542 + 8738

5) 3843 + 6579

6) 4722 + 8186

7) 2419 + 7224

8) 6768 + 3169

9)
$$\begin{array}{r} 4{,}694 \\ +\ 7{,}359 \\ \hline \end{array}$$

10)
$$\begin{array}{r} 9{,}622 \\ +\ 6{,}114 \\ \hline \end{array}$$

11)
$$\begin{array}{r} 1{,}278 \\ +\ 5{,}313 \\ \hline \end{array}$$

12)
$$\begin{array}{r} 8{,}259 \\ +\ 7{,}229 \\ \hline \end{array}$$

Answers of Worksheets – Chapter 1

Adding Whole Numbers

1) 7,845
2) 6,486
3) 8,468
4) 5,801
5) 9,451
6) 8,404
7) 131
8) 1500
9) 1,100
10) 1300
11) 530
12) 1,560
13) $9,355

Subtracting Whole Numbers

1) 3,097
2) 1,891
3) 4,609
4) 2,044
5) 5,461
6) 901
7) 1,103
8) 1,329
9) 546
10) 1,050
11) 1,890
12) 320
13) 1,792

Dividing Whole Numbers

1) 5
2) 10
3) 3
4) 6
5) 3
6) 4
7) 7
8) 5
9) 8
10) 45
11) 6
12) 6
13) 5
14) 5
15) 2
16) 30
17) 30
18) 7

Multiplying Whole Numbers

1) 31,200
2) 12,000
3) 28,080
4) 16,000
5) 12,500
6) 80,000
7) 142,052
8) 240,656
9) 248,898
10) 50,400
11) 68,000
12) 440,000

Rounding Whole Numbers

1) 2000
2) 3000
3) 3360
4) 1280
5) 2360
6) 1330
7) 1200
8) 1460
9) 7500
10) 1910
11) 4240
12) 9000
13) 3450
14) 2600
15) 1200
16) 7700
17) 9290
18) 5240
19) 2490
20) 2900
21) 10,000
22) 4560
23) 6900
24) 9870

Whole Number Estimation

1) 860
2) 4420
3) 11020
4) 10280
5) 10420
6) 12910
7) 9640
8) 9940
9) 12050
10) 15730
11) 6590
12) 15490

Chapter 2: Arithmetic and Number Theory

Topics that you'll learn in this chapter:

- ✓ Simplifying Fractions
- ✓ Adding and Subtracting Fractions
- ✓ Multiplying and Dividing Fractions
- ✓ Adding Mixed Numbers
- ✓ Subtract Mixed Numbers
- ✓ Multiplying Mixed Numbers
- ✓ Dividing Mixed Numbers
- ✓ Comparing Decimals
- ✓ Rounding Decimals
- ✓ Adding and Subtracting Decimals
- ✓ Multiplying and Dividing Decimals
- ✓ Converting Between Fractions, Decimals and Mixed Numbers
- ✓ Factoring Numbers
- ✓ Greatest Common Factor
- ✓ Least Common Multiple
- ✓ Divisibility Rules

Simplifying Fractions

Helpful Hints	– Evenly divide both the top and bottom of the fraction by 2, 3, 5, 7, ... etc. – Continue until you can't go any further.	Example: $\dfrac{4}{12} = \dfrac{2}{6} = \dfrac{1}{3}$

✎ Simplify the fractions.

1) $\dfrac{22}{36}$

2) $\dfrac{8}{10}$

3) $\dfrac{12}{18}$

4) $\dfrac{6}{8}$

5) $\dfrac{13}{39}$

6) $\dfrac{5}{20}$

7) $\dfrac{16}{36}$

8) $\dfrac{18}{36}$

9) $\dfrac{20}{50}$

10) $\dfrac{6}{54}$

11) $\dfrac{45}{81}$

12) $\dfrac{21}{28}$

13) $\dfrac{35}{56}$

14) $\dfrac{52}{64}$

15) $\dfrac{13}{65}$

16) $\dfrac{44}{77}$

17) $\dfrac{21}{42}$

18) $\dfrac{15}{36}$

19) $\dfrac{9}{24}$

20) $\dfrac{20}{80}$

21) $\dfrac{25}{45}$

Adding and Subtracting Fractions

Helpful Hints

− For "like" fractions (fractions with the same denominator), add or subtract the numerators and write the answer over the common denominator.
− Find equivalent fractions with the same denominator before you can add or subtract fractions with different denominators.
− Adding and Subtracting with the same denominator:

$$\frac{a}{b} + \frac{c}{b} = \frac{a+c}{b}$$
$$\frac{a}{b} - \frac{c}{b} = \frac{a-c}{b}$$

− Adding and Subtracting fractions with different denominators:

$$\frac{a}{b} + \frac{c}{d} = \frac{ad+cb}{bd}$$
$$\frac{a}{b} - \frac{c}{d} = \frac{ad-cb}{bd}$$

Add fractions.

1) $\frac{2}{3} + \frac{1}{2}$

2) $\frac{3}{5} + \frac{1}{3}$

3) $\frac{5}{6} + \frac{1}{2}$

4) $\frac{7}{4} + \frac{5}{9}$

5) $\frac{2}{5} + \frac{1}{5}$

6) $\frac{3}{7} + \frac{1}{2}$

7) $\frac{3}{4} + \frac{2}{5}$

8) $\frac{2}{3} + \frac{1}{5}$

9) $\frac{16}{25} + \frac{3}{5}$

Subtract fractions.

10) $\frac{4}{5} - \frac{2}{5}$

11) $\frac{3}{5} - \frac{2}{7}$

12) $\frac{1}{2} - \frac{1}{3}$

13) $\frac{8}{9} - \frac{3}{5}$

14) $\frac{3}{7} - \frac{3}{14}$

15) $\frac{4}{15} - \frac{1}{10}$

16) $\frac{3}{4} - \frac{13}{18}$

17) $\frac{5}{8} - \frac{2}{5}$

18) $\frac{1}{2} - \frac{1}{9}$

Multiplying and Dividing Fractions

Helpful Hints

– **Multiplying fractions:** multiply the top numbers and multiply the bottom numbers.

– **Dividing fractions:** Keep, Change, Flip. Keep first fraction, change division sign to multiplication, and flip the numerator and denominator of the second fraction. Then, solve!

Example:

$$\frac{a}{b} \times \frac{c}{d} = \frac{a \times c}{b \times d}$$

$$\frac{a}{b} \div \frac{c}{d} = \frac{a}{b} \times \frac{d}{c} = \frac{ad}{bc}$$

✎ **Multiplying fractions. Then simplify.**

1) $\dfrac{1}{5} \times \dfrac{2}{3}$

2) $\dfrac{3}{4} \times \dfrac{2}{3}$

3) $\dfrac{2}{5} \times \dfrac{3}{7}$

4) $\dfrac{3}{8} \times \dfrac{1}{3}$

5) $\dfrac{3}{5} \times \dfrac{2}{5}$

6) $\dfrac{7}{9} \times \dfrac{1}{3}$

7) $\dfrac{2}{3} \times \dfrac{3}{8}$

8) $\dfrac{1}{4} \times \dfrac{1}{3}$

9) $\dfrac{5}{7} \times \dfrac{7}{12}$

✎ **Dividing fractions.**

10) $\dfrac{2}{9} \div \dfrac{1}{4}$

11) $\dfrac{1}{2} \div \dfrac{1}{3}$

12) $\dfrac{6}{11} \div \dfrac{3}{4}$

13) $\dfrac{11}{14} \div \dfrac{1}{10}$

14) $\dfrac{3}{5} \div \dfrac{5}{9}$

15) $\dfrac{1}{2} \div \dfrac{1}{2}$

16) $\dfrac{3}{5} \div \dfrac{1}{5}$

17) $\dfrac{12}{21} \div \dfrac{3}{7}$

18) $\dfrac{5}{14} \div \dfrac{9}{10}$

Adding Mixed Numbers

Helpful Hints

Use the following steps for both adding and subtracting mixed numbers.

– Find the Least Common Denominator (LCD)
– Find the equivalent fractions for each mixed number.
– Add fractions after finding common denominator.
– Write your answer in lowest terms.

Example:

$1\frac{3}{4} + 2\frac{3}{8} = 4\frac{1}{8}$

✎ Add.

1) $4\frac{1}{2} + 5\frac{1}{2}$

2) $2\frac{3}{8} + 3\frac{1}{8}$

3) $6\frac{1}{5} + 3\frac{2}{5}$

4) $1\frac{1}{3} + 2\frac{2}{3}$

5) $5\frac{1}{6} + 5\frac{1}{2}$

6) $3\frac{1}{3} + 1\frac{1}{3}$

7) $1\frac{10}{11} + 1\frac{1}{3}$

8) $2\frac{3}{6} + 1\frac{1}{2}$

9) $5\frac{3}{5} + 5\frac{1}{5}$

10) $7 + \frac{1}{5}$

11) $1\frac{5}{7} + \frac{1}{3}$

12) $2\frac{1}{4} + 1\frac{1}{2}$

Subtract Mixed Numbers

> **Helpful Hints**
>
> Use the following steps for both adding and subtracting mixed numbers.
>
> Find the Least Common Denominator (LCD)
> – Find the equivalent fractions for each mixed number.
> – Add or subtract fractions after finding common denominator.
> – Write your answer in lowest terms.
>
> Example:
>
> $5\frac{2}{3} - 3\frac{2}{7} = 2\frac{8}{21}$

✎ Subtract.

1) $4\frac{1}{2} - 3\frac{1}{2}$

2) $3\frac{3}{8} - 3\frac{1}{8}$

3) $6\frac{3}{5} - 5\frac{1}{5}$

4) $2\frac{1}{3} - 1\frac{2}{3}$

5) $6\frac{1}{6} - 5\frac{1}{2}$

6) $3\frac{1}{3} - 1\frac{1}{3}$

7) $2\frac{10}{11} - 1\frac{1}{3}$

8) $2\frac{1}{2} - 1\frac{1}{2}$

9) $6\frac{3}{5} - 2\frac{1}{5}$

10) $7\frac{2}{5} - 1\frac{1}{5}$

11) $2\frac{5}{7} - 1\frac{1}{3}$

12) $2\frac{1}{4} - 1\frac{1}{2}$

Multiplying Mixed Numbers

Helpful Hints

1- Convert the mixed numbers to improper fractions.
2- Multiply fractions and simplify if necessary.

$$a\frac{c}{b} = a + \frac{c}{b} = \frac{ab+c}{b}$$

Example:

$$2\frac{1}{3} \times 5\frac{3}{7} =$$

$$\frac{7}{3} \times \frac{38}{7} = \frac{38}{3} = 12\frac{2}{3}$$

✎ *Find each product.*

1) $1\frac{2}{3} \times 1\frac{1}{4}$

2) $1\frac{3}{5} \times 1\frac{2}{3}$

3) $1\frac{2}{3} \times 3\frac{2}{7}$

4) $4\frac{1}{8} \times 1\frac{2}{5}$

5) $2\frac{2}{5} \times 3\frac{1}{5}$

6) $1\frac{1}{3} \times 1\frac{2}{3}$

7) $1\frac{5}{8} \times 2\frac{1}{2}$

8) $3\frac{2}{5} \times 2\frac{1}{5}$

9) $2\frac{2}{3} \times 4\frac{1}{4}$

10) $2\frac{3}{5} \times 1\frac{2}{4}$

11) $1\frac{1}{3} \times 1\frac{1}{4}$

12) $3\frac{2}{5} \times 1\frac{1}{5}$

Dividing Mixed Numbers

Helpful Hints

1- Convert the mixed numbers to improper fractions.
2- Divide fractions and simplify if necessary.

$$a\frac{c}{b} = a + \frac{c}{b} = \frac{ab+c}{b}$$

Example:

$$2\frac{1}{3} \times 5\frac{3}{7} =$$

$$\frac{7}{3} \times \frac{38}{7} = \frac{38}{3} = 12\frac{2}{3}$$

✏️ *Find each quotient.*

1) $2\frac{1}{5} \div 2\frac{1}{2}$

2) $2\frac{3}{5} \div 1\frac{1}{3}$

3) $3\frac{1}{6} \div 4\frac{2}{3}$

4) $1\frac{2}{3} \div 3\frac{1}{3}$

5) $4\frac{1}{8} \div 2\frac{2}{4}$

6) $3\frac{1}{2} \div 2\frac{3}{5}$

7) $3\frac{5}{9} \div 1\frac{2}{5}$

8) $2\frac{2}{7} \div 1\frac{1}{2}$

9) $3\frac{1}{5} \div 1\frac{1}{2}$

10) $4\frac{3}{5} \div 2\frac{1}{3}$

11) $6\frac{1}{6} \div 1\frac{2}{3}$

12) $2\frac{2}{3} \div 1\frac{1}{3}$

Comparing Decimals

> *Helpful Hints*
> - **Decimals:** is a fraction written in a special form. For example, instead of writing $\frac{1}{2}$ you can write 0.5.
> - **For comparing:**
>   Equal to =
>   Less than <
>   Greater than >
>   Greater than or equal ≥
>   Less than or equal ≤
>
> **Example:**
>
> 2.67 > 0.267

✍ *Write the correct comparison symbol (>, < or =).*

1) 1.25   2.3
2) 0.5   0.23
3) 3.2   3.2
4) 4.58   45.8
5) 2.75   0.275
6) 5.2   5
7) 3.1   0.31
8) 6.33   0.733

9) 8   0.8
10) 4.56 0.456
11) 1.12 1.14
12) 2.77 2.78
13) 6.08 6.11
14) 1.11 0.211
15) 2.6   2.55
16) 1.24 1.25

17) 5.52 0.552
18) 0.33 0.033
19) 14.4 14.4
20) 0.05 0.50
21) 0.59 0.7
22) 0.5   0.05
23) 0.90 0.9
24) 0.27 0.4

Rounding Decimals

Helpful Hints

We can round decimals to a certain accuracy or number of decimal places. This is used to make calculation easier to do and results easier to understand, when exact values are not too important.

First, you'll need to remember your place values:

Example:

$\underline{6}.37 = 6$

12.4567

1: tens   2: ones   4: tenths

5: hundredths   6: thousandths   7: ten thousandths

✎ Round each decimal number to the nearest place indicated.

1) 0.2<u>3</u>

2) 4.0<u>4</u>

3) 5.<u>6</u>23

4) 0.2<u>6</u>6

5) <u>6</u>.37

6) 0.<u>8</u>8

7) 8.<u>2</u>4

8) <u>7</u>.0760

9) 1.6<u>2</u>9

10) 6.<u>3</u>959

11) <u>1</u>.9

12) <u>5</u>.2167

13) 5.<u>8</u>63

14) 8.<u>5</u>4

15) 8<u>0</u>.69

16) 6<u>5</u>.85

17) 70.<u>7</u>8

18) 61<u>5</u>.755

19) 1<u>6</u>.4

20) 9<u>5</u>.81

21) <u>2</u>.408

22) 7<u>6</u>.3

23) 116.<u>5</u>14

24) 8.<u>0</u>6

Adding and Subtracting Decimals

| Helpful Hints | 1– Line up the numbers.

2– Add zeros to have same number of digits for both numbers.

3– Add or Subtract using column addition or subtraction. | Example:

  16.18
− 13.45
   2.73 |

✎ *Add and subtract decimals.*

1)   15.14
   − 12.18
   ─────

2)   65.72
   + 43.67
   ─────

3)   82.56
   + 12.28
   ─────

4)   34.18
   − 23.45
   ─────

5)   90.37
   + 56.97
   ─────

6)   45.78
   − 23.39
   ─────

✎ *Solve.*

7) ____ + 1.3 = 4.8

8) 4.2 + ____ = 11.6

9) 9.9 + ____ = 16

10) 6.9 + ____ = 16.4

11) ____ + 5.1 = 8.6

12) ____ + 7.9 = 15.2

Multiplying and Dividing Decimals

> *Helpful Hints*
>
> **For Multiplication:**
>
> — Set up and multiply the numbers as you do with whole numbers.
>
> — Count the total number of decimal places in both of the factors.
>
> — Place the decimal point in the product.
>
> **For Division:**
>
> — If the divisor is not a whole number, move decimal point to right to make it a whole number. Do the same for dividend.
>
> — Divide similar to whole numbers.

✎ **Find each product.**

1) 4.5 × 1.6

2) 7.7 × 9.9

3) 2.6 × 1.5

4) 8.9 × 9.7

5) 15.1 × 12.6

6) 6.9 × 3.3

7) 5.7 × 7.8

8) 98.20 × 100

9) 23.99 × 1000

✎ **Find each quotient.**

10) 9.2 ÷ 3.6

11) 27.6 ÷ 3.8

12) 12.6 ÷ 4.7

13) 6.5 ÷ 8.1

14) 1.4 ÷ 10

15) 3.6 ÷ 100

16) 4.24 ÷ 10

17) 14.6 ÷ 100

18) 1.8 ÷ 1000

Converting Between Fractions, Decimals and Mixed Numbers

Helpful Hints

Fraction to Decimal:

– Divide the top number by the bottom number.

Decimal to Fraction:

– Write decimal over 1.

– Multiply both top and bottom by 10 for every digit on the right side of the decimal point.

– Simplify.

✍ **Convert fractions to decimals.**

1) $\dfrac{9}{10}$

2) $\dfrac{56}{100}$

3) $\dfrac{3}{4}$

4) $\dfrac{2}{5}$

5) $\dfrac{3}{9}$

6) $\dfrac{40}{50}$

7) $\dfrac{12}{10}$

8) $\dfrac{8}{5}$

9) $\dfrac{69}{10}$

✍ **Convert decimal into fraction or mixed numbers.**

10) 0.3

11) 4.5

12) 2.5

13) 2.3

14) 0.8

15) 0.25

16) 0.14

17) 0.2

18) 0.08

19) 0.45

20) 2.6

21) 5.2

Factoring Numbers

Helpful	- Factoring numbers means to break the numbers into their prime factors.	**Example:**
Hints	- First few prime numbers: 2, 3, 5, 7, 11, 13, 17, 19	$12 = 2 \times 2 \times 3$

✎ **List all positive factors of each number.**

1) 68   6) 78   11) 54

2) 56   7) 50   12) 28

3) 24   8) 98   13) 55

4) 40   9) 45   14) 85

5) 86   10) 26   15) 48

✎ **List the prime factorization for each number.**

16) 50   19) 21   22) 26

17) 25   20) 45   23) 86

18) 69   21) 68   24) 93

Greatest Common Factor

Helpful Hints

- List the prime factors of each number.
- Multiply common prime factors.

Example:

$200 = 2 \times 2 \times 2 \times 5 \times 5$

$60 = 2 \times 2 \times 3 \times 5$

GCF (200, 60) = $2 \times 2 \times 5 = 20$

✎ Find the GCF for each number pair.

1) 20, 30

2) 4, 14

3) 5, 45

4) 68, 12

5) 5, 12

6) 15, 27

7) 3, 24

8) 34, 6

9) 4, 10

10) 5, 3

11) 6, 16

12) 30, 3

13) 24, 28

14) 70, 10

15) 45, 8

16) 90, 35

17) 78, 34

18) 55, 75

19) 60, 72

20) 100, 78

21) 30, 40

Least Common Multiple

Helpful Hints

- Find the GCF for the two numbers.
- Divide that GCF into either number.
- Take that answer and multiply it by the other number.

Example:

LCM (200, 60):

GCF is 20

200 ÷ 20 = 10

10 × 60 = 600

✏️ Find the LCM for each number pair.

1) 4, 14

2) 5, 15

3) 16, 10

4) 4, 34

5) 8, 3

6) 12, 24

7) 9, 18

8) 5, 6

9) 8, 19

10) 9, 21

11) 19, 29

12) 7, 6

13) 25, 6

14) 4, 8

15) 30, 10, 50

16) 18, 36, 27

17) 12, 8, 18

18) 8, 18, 4

19) 26, 20, 30

20) 10, 4, 24

21) 15, 30, 45

Divisibility Rules

Helpful Hints	- Divisibility means that a number can be divided by other numbers evenly.	Example: 24 is divisible by 6, because 24 ÷ 6 = 4

✎ *Use the divisibility rules to find the factors of each number.*

      8   <u>2</u> 3 <u>4</u> 5 6 7 <u>8</u> 9 10

1) 16   2 3 4 5 6 7 8 9 10

2) 10   2 3 4 5 6 7 8 9 10

3) 15   2 3 4 5 6 7 8 9 10

4) 28   2 3 4 5 6 7 8 9 10

5) 36   2 3 4 5 6 7 8 9 10

6) 15   2 3 4 5 6 7 8 9 10

7) 27   2 3 4 5 6 7 8 9 10

8) 70   2 3 4 5 6 7 8 9 10

9) 57   2 3 4 5 6 7 8 9 10

10) 102   2 3 4 5 6 7 8 9 10

11) 144   2 3 4 5 6 7 8 9 10

12) 75   2 3 4 5 6 7 8 9 10

Test Preparation

1) Mr. Jones saves $2,500 out of his monthly family income of $55,000. What fractional part of his income does he save?

   A. $\frac{1}{22}$

   B. $\frac{1}{11}$

   C. $\frac{3}{25}$

   D. $\frac{2}{15}$

2) What is the missing prime factor of number 360?

   $360 = 2^3 \times 3^2 \times \underline{}$

   Write your answer in the box below.

3) Which list shows the fractions in order from least to greatest?

$$\frac{2}{3}, \frac{5}{7}, \frac{3}{10}, \frac{1}{2}, \frac{6}{13}$$

A. $\frac{2}{3}, \frac{5}{7}, \frac{3}{10}, \frac{1}{2}, \frac{6}{13}$

B. $\frac{6}{13}, \frac{1}{2}, \frac{2}{3}, \frac{5}{7}, \frac{3}{10}$

C. $\frac{3}{10}, \frac{2}{3}, \frac{5}{7}, \frac{1}{2}, \frac{6}{13}$

D. $\frac{3}{10}, \frac{6}{13}, \frac{1}{2}, \frac{2}{3}, \frac{5}{7}$

4) Which statement about 5 multiplied by $\frac{2}{3}$ is true?

A. The product is between 2 and 3.

B. The product is between 3 and 4

C. The product is more than $\frac{11}{3}$.

D. The product is between $\frac{14}{3}$ and 5.

5) Which list shows the fractions listed in order from least to greatest?

$$\frac{1}{6} \quad \frac{1}{8} \quad \frac{1}{3} \quad \frac{1}{10}$$

A. $\quad \frac{1}{3} \quad \frac{1}{6} \quad \frac{1}{8} \quad \frac{1}{10}$

B. $\quad \frac{1}{8} \quad \frac{1}{3} \quad \frac{1}{10} \quad \frac{1}{6}$

C. $\quad \frac{1}{6} \quad \frac{1}{10} \quad \frac{1}{3} \quad \frac{1}{8}$

D. $\quad \frac{1}{10} \quad \frac{1}{8} \quad \frac{1}{6} \quad \frac{1}{3}$

6) $[6 \times (-24) + 8] - (-4) + [4 \times 5] \div 2 = ?$

Write your answer in the box below.

7) Four one – foot rulers can be split among how many users to leave each with $\frac{1}{6}$ of a ruler?

   A. 4

   B. 6

   C. 12

   D. 24

8) Last week 24,000 fans attended a football match. This week three times as many bought tickets, but one sixth of them cancelled their tickets. How many are attending this week?

   A. 48,000

   B. 54,000

   C. 60,000

   D. 72,000

9) What is the missing prime factor of number 180?

   $180 = 2^2 \times 3^2 \times \underline{}$

   A. 2

   B. 3

   C. 5

   D. 6

10) A rope 10 yards long is cut into 4 equal parts. Which expression does NOT equal to the length of each part?

A. $10 \div 4$

B. $\frac{10}{4}$

C. $4 \div 10$

D. $4\overline{)10}$

Answers of Worksheets – Chapter 2

Simplifying Fractions

1) $\frac{11}{18}$
2) $\frac{4}{5}$
3) $\frac{2}{3}$
4) $\frac{3}{4}$
5) $\frac{1}{3}$
6) $\frac{1}{4}$
7) $\frac{4}{9}$
8) $\frac{1}{2}$
9) $\frac{2}{5}$
10) $\frac{1}{9}$
11) $\frac{5}{9}$
12) $\frac{3}{4}$
13) $\frac{5}{8}$
14) $\frac{13}{16}$
15) $\frac{1}{5}$
16) $\frac{4}{7}$
17) $\frac{1}{2}$
18) $\frac{5}{12}$
19) $\frac{3}{8}$
20) $\frac{1}{4}$
21) $\frac{5}{9}$

Adding and Subtracting Fractions

1) $\frac{7}{6}$
2) $\frac{14}{15}$
3) $\frac{4}{3}$
4) $\frac{83}{36}$
5) $\frac{3}{5}$
6) $\frac{13}{14}$
7) $\frac{23}{20}$
8) $\frac{13}{15}$
9) $\frac{31}{25}$
10) $\frac{2}{5}$
11) $\frac{11}{35}$
12) $\frac{1}{6}$
13) $\frac{13}{45}$
14) $\frac{3}{14}$
15) $\frac{1}{6}$
16) $\frac{1}{36}$
17) $\frac{9}{40}$
18) $\frac{7}{18}$

Multiplying and Dividing Fractions

1) $\dfrac{2}{15}$

2) $\dfrac{1}{2}$

3) $\dfrac{6}{35}$

4) $\dfrac{1}{8}$

5) $\dfrac{6}{25}$

6) $\dfrac{7}{27}$

7) $\dfrac{1}{4}$

8) $\dfrac{1}{12}$

9) $\dfrac{5}{12}$

10) $\dfrac{8}{9}$

11) $\dfrac{3}{2}$

12) $\dfrac{8}{11}$

13) $\dfrac{55}{7}$

14) $\dfrac{27}{25}$

15) 1

16) 3

17) $\dfrac{4}{3}$

18) $\dfrac{25}{63}$

Adding Mixed Numbers

1) 10

2) $5\dfrac{1}{2}$

3) $9\dfrac{3}{5}$

4) 4

5) $10\dfrac{2}{3}$

6) $4\dfrac{2}{3}$

7) $3\dfrac{8}{33}$

8) 4

9) $10\dfrac{4}{5}$

10) $7\dfrac{1}{5}$

11) $2\dfrac{1}{21}$

12) $3\dfrac{3}{4}$

Subtract Mixed Numbers

1) 1

2) $\dfrac{1}{4}$

3) $1\dfrac{2}{5}$

4) $\dfrac{2}{3}$

5) $\dfrac{2}{3}$

6) 2

7) $1\dfrac{19}{33}$

8) 1

9) $4\dfrac{2}{5}$

10) $6\dfrac{1}{5}$

11) $1\dfrac{8}{21}$

12) $\dfrac{3}{4}$

Multiplying Mixed Numbers

1) $2\frac{1}{12}$
2) $2\frac{2}{3}$
3) $5\frac{10}{21}$
4) $5\frac{31}{40}$
5) $7\frac{17}{25}$
6) $2\frac{2}{9}$
7) $4\frac{1}{16}$
8) $7\frac{12}{25}$
9) $11\frac{1}{3}$
10) $3\frac{9}{10}$
11) $1\frac{2}{3}$
12) $4\frac{2}{25}$

Dividing Mixed Numbers

1) $\frac{22}{25}$
2) $1\frac{19}{20}$
3) $\frac{19}{28}$
4) $\frac{1}{2}$
5) $1\frac{13}{20}$
6) $1\frac{9}{26}$
7) $2\frac{34}{63}$
8) $1\frac{11}{21}$
9) $2\frac{2}{15}$
10) $1\frac{34}{35}$
11) $3\frac{7}{10}$
12) 2

Comparing Decimals

1) 1.25 < 2.3
2) 0.5 > 0.23
3) 3.2 = 3.2
4) 4.58 < 45.8
5) 2.75 > 0.275
6) 5.2 > 5
7) 3.1 > 0.31
8) 6.33 > 0.733
9) 8 > 0.8
10) 4.56 > 0.456
11) 1.12 < 1.14
12) 2.77 < 2.78
13) 6.08 < 6.11
14) 1.11 > 0.211
15) 2.6 > 2.55
16) 1.24 < 1.25
17) 5.52 > 0.552
18) 0.33 > 0.033
19) 14.4 = 14.4
20) 0.05 < 0.50
21) 0.59 < 0.7
22) 0.5 > 0.05
23) 0.90 = 0.9
24) 0.27 < 0.4

Rounding Decimals

1) 0.2
2) 4.0
3) 5.6
4) 0.3
5) 6
6) 0.9
7) 8.2
8) 7
9) 1.63
10) 6.4
11) 2
12) 5
13) 5.9
14) 8.5
15) 81
16) 66
17) 70.8
18) 616
19) 16
20) 96
21) 2
22) 76
23) 116.5
24) 8.1

Adding and Subtracting Decimals

1) 2.96
2) 109.39
3) 94.84
4) 10.73
5) 147.34
6) 22.39
7) 3.5
8) 7.4
9) 6.1
10) 9.5
11) 3.5
12) 7.3

Multiplying and Dividing Decimals

1) 7.2
2) 76.23
3) 3.9
4) 86.33
5) 190.26
6) 22.77
7) 44.46
8) 9820
9) 23990
10) 2.5555…
11) 7.2631…
12) 2.6808…
13) 0.8024…
14) 0.14
15) 0.036
16) 0.424
17) 0.146
18) 0.0018

Converting Between Fractions, Decimals and Mixed Numbers

1) 0.9
2) 0.56
3) 0.75
4) 0.4
5) 0.333…
6) 0.8
7) 1.2
8) 1.6
9) 6.9
10) $\frac{3}{10}$
11) $4\frac{1}{2}$
12) $2\frac{1}{2}$

13) $2\frac{3}{10}$
14) $\frac{4}{5}$
15) $\frac{1}{4}$
16) $\frac{7}{50}$
17) $\frac{1}{5}$
18) $\frac{2}{25}$
19) $\frac{9}{20}$
20) $2\frac{3}{5}$
21) $5\frac{1}{5}$

Factoring Numbers

1) 1, 2, 4, 17, 34, 68
2) 1, 2, 4, 7, 8, 14, 28, 56
3) 1, 2, 3, 4, 6, 8, 12, 24
4) 1, 2, 4, 5, 8, 10, 20, 40
5) 1, 2, 43, 86
6) 1, 2, 3, 6, 13, 26, 39, 78
7) 1, 2, 5, 10, 25, 50
8) 1, 2, 7, 14, 49, 98
9) 1, 3, 5, 9, 15, 45
10) 1, 2, 13, 26
11) 1, 2, 3, 6, 9, 18, 27, 54
12) 1, 2, 4, 7, 14, 28

13) 1, 5, 11, 55
14) 1, 5, 17, 85
15) 1, 2, 3, 4, 6, 8, 12, 16, 24, 48
16) 2 × 5 × 5
17) 5 × 5
18) 3 × 23
19) 3 × 7
20) 3 × 3 × 5
21) 2 × 2 × 17
22) 2 × 13
23) 2 × 43
24) 3 × 31

Greatest Common Factor

1) 10
2) 2
3) 5
4) 4
5) 1
6) 3
7) 3
8) 2
9) 2
10) 1
11) 2
12) 3
13) 4
14) 10
15) 1
16) 5
17) 2
18) 5
19) 12
20) 2
21) 10

Least Common Multiple

1) 28
2) 15
3) 80
4) 68
5) 24
6) 24
7) 18
8) 30
9) 152
10) 63
11) 551
12) 42
13) 150
14) 8
15) 150

16)	108	18) 72		20)	120
17)	72	19) 780		21)	90

Divisibility Rules

1) 16   <u>2</u> 3 <u>4</u> 5 6 7 <u>8</u> 9 10

2) 10   <u>2</u> 3 4 <u>5</u> 6 7 8 9 <u>10</u>

3) 15   2 <u>3</u> 4 <u>5</u> 6 7 8 9 10

4) 28   <u>2</u> 3 <u>4</u> 5 6 <u>7</u> 8 9 10

5) 36   <u>2</u> <u>3</u> <u>4</u> 5 <u>6</u> 7 8 <u>9</u> 10

6) 18   <u>2</u> <u>3</u> 4 5 <u>6</u> 7 8 <u>9</u> 10

7) 27   2 <u>3</u> 4 5 6 7 8 <u>9</u> 10

8) 70   <u>2</u> 3 4 <u>5</u> 6 <u>7</u> 8 9 <u>10</u>

9) 57   2 <u>3</u> 4 5 6 7 8 9 10

10) 102   <u>2</u> <u>3</u> 4 5 <u>6</u> 7 8 9 10

11) 144   <u>2</u> <u>3</u> <u>4</u> 5 <u>6</u> 7 <u>8</u> <u>9</u> 10

12) 75   2 <u>3</u> 4 <u>5</u> 6 7 8 9 10

Test Preparation Answers

1) Choice A is correct

2,500 out of 55,000 equals to $\frac{2500}{55000} = \frac{25}{550} = \frac{1}{22}$

2) The answer is 5^1.

Let x be the number of blank.

$360 = 2 \times 2 \times 2 \times 3 \times 3 \times x \Rightarrow x = \frac{360}{72} \Rightarrow x = 5$

3) Choice D is correct.

Compare each fraction, then we have:

$\frac{3}{10} < \frac{6}{13} < \frac{1}{2} < \frac{2}{3} < \frac{5}{7}$

4) Choice B is correct

To find the discount, multiply the 5 by $\frac{2}{3}$. Therefore we have $\frac{10}{3}$

After simplification now we have $3\frac{1}{3}$, that is between 3 and 4.

5) Choice D is correct

In fractions as much as denominators grow up, fraction decrease and as much as numerators grow up, fraction increase. So the least one of this list is: $\frac{1}{10}$ and the greatest one of this list is: $\frac{1}{3}$

6) The answer is: – 122

Use PEMDAS (order of operation):

$[6 \times (-24) + 8] - (-4) + [4 \times 5] \div 2 = [-144 + 8] - (-4) + [20] \div 2 =$

$[-144 + 8] - (-4) + 10 =$

$[-136] - (-4) + 10 = [-136] + 4 + 10 = -122$

7) Choice D is correct

$4 \div \dfrac{1}{6} = 24$

8) Choice C is correct

Three times of 24,000 is 72,000. One sixth of them cancelled their tickets.

One sixth of 72,000 equals 12,000 (1/6 × 72000 = 12000).

60,000 (72000 – 12000 = 60000) fans are attending this week

9) Choice C is correct

Let x be the missed number.

$180 = 4 \times 9 \times x \Rightarrow x = 5$

10) Choice C is correct.

All other options show 10 divided by 4. Option C is 4 divided by 10.

Chapter 3: Real Numbers and Integers

Topics that you'll learn in this chapter:

- ✓ Adding and Subtracting Integers
- ✓ Multiplying and Dividing Integers
- ✓ Ordering Integers and Numbers
- ✓ Arrange, Order, and Comparing Integers
- ✓ Order of Operations
- ✓ Mixed Integer Computations
- ✓ Absolute Value
- ✓ Integers and Absolute Value
- ✓ Classifying Real Numbers Venn Diagram

Adding and Subtracting Integers

Helpful Hints

- **Integers:** {... , –3, –2, –1, 0, 1, 2, 3, ...}
  Includes: zero, counting numbers, and the negative of the counting numbers.
- Add a positive integer by moving to the right on the number line.
- Add a negative integer by moving to the left on the number line.
- Subtract an integer by adding its opposite.

Example:

12 + 10 = 22

25 – 13 = 12

(–24) + 12 = –12

(–14) + (–12) = –26

14 – (–13) = 27

✎ Find the sum.

1) (– 12) + (– 4)

2) 5 + (– 24)

3) (– 14) + 23

4) (– 8) + (39)

5) 43 + (–12)

6) (– 23) + (– 4) + 3

7) 4 + (– 12) + (– 10) + (– 25)

8) 19 + (– 15) + 25 + 11

9) (– 9) + (– 12) + (32 – 14)

10) 4 + (– 30) + (45 – 34)

✎ Find the difference.

11) (– 14) – (– 9) – (18)

12) (– 9) – (– 25)

13) (– 12) – (8)

14) (28) – (– 4)

15) (34) – (2)

16) (55) – (– 5) + (– 4)

17) (9) – (2) – (– 5)

18) (2) – (4) – (– 15)

19) (23) – (4) – (– 34)

20) (– 45) – (– 87)

Multiplying and Dividing Integers

Helpful Hints

(negative) × (negative) = positive
(negative) ÷ (negative) = positive
(negative) × (positive) = negative
(negative) ÷ (positive) = negative
(positive) × (positive) = positive

Examples:

$3 \times 2 = 6$
$3 \times -3 = -9$
$-2 \times -2 = 4$
$10 \div 2 = 5$
$-4 \div 2 = -2$
$-12 \div -6 = 3$

✏ Find each product.

1) $(-8) \times (-2)$
2) 3×6
3) $(-4) \times 5 \times (-6)$
4) $2 \times (-6) \times (-6)$
5) $11 \times (-12)$

6) $10 \times (-5)$
7) 8×8
8) $(-8) \times (-9)$
9) $6 \times (-5) \times 3$
10) $6 \times (-1) \times 2$

✏ Find each quotient.

11) $18 \div 3$
12) $(-24) \div 4$
13) $(-63) \div (-9)$
14) $54 \div 9$
15) $20 \div (-2)$

16) $(-66) \div (-11)$
17) $64 \div 8$
18) $(-121) \div 11$
19) $72 \div 9$
20) $16 \div 4$

Ordering Integers and Numbers

Helpful Hints

To compare numbers, you can use number line! As you move from left to right on the number line, you find a bigger number!

Example:

Order integers from least to greatest.

$(-11, -13, 7, -2, 12)$

$-13 < -11 < -2 < 7 < 12$

✎ Order each set of integers from least to greatest.

1) $-15, -19, 20, -4, 1$ ___, ___, ___, ___, ___, ___

2) $6, -5, 4, -3, 2$ ___, ___, ___, ___, ___, ___

3) $15, -42, 19, 0, -22$ ___, ___, ___, ___, ___, ___

4) $26, -91, 0, -13, 67, -55$ ___, ___, ___, ___, ___, ___

5) $-17, -71, 90, -25, -54, -39$ ___, ___, ___, ___, ___, ___

6) $98, 5, 46, 19, 77, 24$ ___, ___, ___, ___, ___, ___

✎ Order each set of integers from greatest to least.

7) $-2, 5, -3, 6, -4$ ___, ___, ___, ___, ___, ___

8) $-37, 7, -17, 27, 47$ ___, ___, ___, ___, ___, ___

9) $32, -27, 19, -17, 15$ ___, ___, ___, ___, ___, ___

10) $68, 81, 21, -18, 94, 72$ ___, ___, ___, ___, ___, ___

Arrange, Order, and Comparing Integers

Helpful Hints

When using a number line, numbers increase as you move to the right.

Examples:

$5 < 7$,

$-5 < -2$

$-18 < -12$

✎ *Arrange these integers in descending order.*

1) 21, 71, −18, −10, 82   ___, ___, ___, ___, ___, ___

2) 15, 11, 20, 12, −9, −5   ___, ___, ___, ___, ___, ___

3) −5, 20, 15, 9, −11   ___, ___, ___, ___, ___, ___

4) 19, 18, −9, −6, −11   ___, ___, ___, ___, ___, ___

5) 56, −34, −12, −5, 32   ___, ___, ___, ___, ___, ___

✎ *Compare. Use >, =, <*

6) −8 ____ 12   11) −56 ____ −58

7) −10 ____ −16   12) 78 ____ 87

8) 43 ____ 34   13) −92 ____ −102

9) 15 ____ −16   14) −12 ____ −12

10) −354 ____ −345   15) −721 ____ −821

Order of Operations

Helpful Hints	- Use "order of operations" rule when there are more than one math operation. - PEMDAS (parentheses / exponents / multiply / divide / add / subtract)	**Example:** $(12 + 4) \div (-4) = -4$

✎ *Evaluate each expression.*

1) $(2 \times 2) + 5$

2) $24 - (3 \times 3)$

3) $(6 \times 4) + 8$

4) $25 - (4 \times 2)$

5) $(6 \times 5) + 3$

6) $64 - (2 \times 4)$

7) $25 + (1 \times 8)$

8) $(6 \times 7) + 7$

9) $48 \div (4 + 4)$

10) $(7 + 11) \div (-2)$

11) $9 + (2 \times 5) + 10$

12) $(5 + 8) \times \frac{3}{5} + 2$

13) $2 \times 7 - (\frac{10}{9-4})$

14) $(12 + 2 - 5) \times 7 - 1$

15) $(\frac{7}{5-1}) \times (2 + 6) \times 2$

16) $20 \div (4 - (10 - 8))$

17) $\frac{50}{4(5-4)-3}$

18) $2 + (8 \times 2)$

Mixed Integer Computations

Helpful Hints	It worth remembering: (negative) × (negative) = positive (negative) ÷ (negative) = positive (negative) × (positive) = negative (negative) ÷ (positive) = negative (positive) × (positive) = positive	Example: (−5) + 6 = 1 (−3) × (−2) = 6 (9) ÷ (−3) = − 3

✎ *Compute.*

1) $(-70) \div (-5)$

2) $(-14) \times 3$

3) $(-4) \times (-15)$

4) $(-65) \div 5$

5) $18 \times (-7)$

6) $(-12) \times (-2)$

7) $\dfrac{(-60)}{(-20)}$

8) $24 \div (-8)$

9) $22 \div (-11)$

10) $\dfrac{(-27)}{3}$

11) $4 \times (-4)$

12) $\dfrac{(-48)}{12}$

13) $(-14) \times (-2)$

14) $(-7) \times (7)$

15) $\dfrac{-30}{-6}$

16) $(-54) \div 6$

17) $(-60) \div (-5)$

18) $(-7) \times (-12)$

19) $(-14) \times 5$

20) $88 \div (-8)$

Absolute Value

Helpful Hints

Refers to the distance of a number from 0, the distances are positive. Therefore, absolute value of a number cannot be negative. $|-22| = 22$

Example:

$|12| \times |-2| = 24$

$$|x| = \begin{cases} x & \text{for } x \geq 0 \\ -x & \text{for } x < 0 \end{cases}$$

$|x| < n \Rightarrow -n < x < n$

$|x| > n \Rightarrow x < -n \text{ or } x > n$

✎ Evaluate.

1) $|-4| + |-12| - 7$

2) $|-5| + |-13|$

3) $-18 + |-5 + 3| - 8$

4) $|27| \div |9|$

5) $|-9| \div |-1|$

6) $|200| \div |-100|$

7) $|55| \div |11|$

8) $|36| \div |-6|$

9) $|25| \times |-5|$

10) $|-3| \times |-8|$

11) $|12| \times |-5|$

12) $|11| \times |-6|$

13) $|-8| \times |4|$

14) $|-9| \times |-7|$

15) $|43 - 67 + 9| + |-11| - 1$

16) $|-45 + 78| + |23| - |45|$

17) $75 + |-11 - 30| - |2|$

18) $|-3 + 15| + |9 + 4| - 1$

Integers and Absolute Value

Helpful Hints

To find an absolute value of a number, just find it's distance from 0!

Example:

$|-6| = 6$

$|6| = 6$

$|-12| = 12$

$|12| = 12$

✎ *Write absolute value of each number.*

1) −4
2) −7
3) −8
4) 4
5) 5
6) −10
7) 1
8) 6
9) 8
10) −2
11) −1
12) 10
13) 3
14) 7
15) −5
16) −3
17) −9
18) 2
19) 4
20) −6
21) 9

✎ *Evaluate.*

22) $|-43| - |12| + 10$
23) $76 + |-15 - 45| - |3|$
24) $30 + |-62| - 46$
25) $|32| - |-78| + 90$
26) $|-35 + 4| + 6 - 4$
27) $|-4| + |-11|$
28) $|-6 + 3 - 4| + |7 + 7|$
29) $|-9| + |-19| - 5$

Classifying Real Numbers Venn Diagram

Helpful Hints

Example:
0.25 =
rational number
and
real number

Natural numbers (counting numbers): are the numbers that are used for counting. 1, 2, 3, …, 100, … are natural numbers.

Whole numbers are the natural numbers plus zero.

Integers include all whole numbers plus "negatives" of the natural numbers.

Rational numbers are numbers that can be written as a fraction. Both top and bottom numbers must be integers.

Irrational numbers are all numbers which cannot be written as fractions.

Real numbers include both the rational and irrational numbers.

✎ *Identify all of the subsets of real number system to which each number belongs.*

Example:

0.1259 : Rational number

$\sqrt{2}$: Irrational number

3 : Natural number, whole number, Integer, rational number

1) 0
2) −5
3) −8.5
4) $\sqrt{4}$
5) −10
6) 18
7) 6
8) π
9) $1\frac{2}{7}$
10) −1
11) $\sqrt{5}$

Test Preparation

1) Which expression has a value of (− 18)?

   A. 8 − (− 4) + (−15) × 2

   B. 12 + (− 3) × (− 2)

   C. − 6 × (− 6) × (− 2) ÷ (− 4)

   D. (− 2) × (− 7) + 4

2) 4 + 8 × (3) − [8 + 8 × 5] ÷ 6 = ?

   Write your answer in the box below.

Answers of Worksheets – Chapter 3

Adding and Subtracting Integers

1) −16
2) −19
3) 9
4) 31
5) 31
6) −24
7) −43
8) 40
9) −3
10) −15
11) −23
12) 16
13) −20
14) 32
15) 32
16) 56
17) 12
18) 13
19) 53
20) 42

Multiplying and Dividing Integers

1) 16
2) 18
3) 120
4) 72
5) −132
6) −50
7) 64
8) 72
9) −90
10) −12
11) 6
12) −6
13) 7
14) 6
15) −10
16) 6
17) 8
18) −11
19) 8
20) 4

Ordering Integers and Numbers

1) −19, −15, −4, 1, 20
2) −5, −3, 2, 4, 6
3) −42, −22, 0, 15, 19
4) −91, −55, −13, 0, 26, 67
5) −71, −54, −39, −25, −17, 90
6) 5, 19, 24, 46, 77, 98
7) 6, 5, −2, −3, −4
8) 47, 27, 7, −17, −37
9) 32, 19, 15, −17, −27
10) 94, 81, 72, 68, 21, −18

Arrange and Order, Comparing Integers

1) 82, 71, 21, − 10, − 18
2) 20, 15, 12, 11, − 5, − 9
3) 20, 15, 9, − 5, −11
4) 19, 18, − 6, − 9, − 11
5) 56, 32, − 5, − 12, − 34
6) <
7) >
8) >
9) >
10) <
11) >
12) <
13) >
14) =
15) >

Order of Operations

1) 9
2) 15
3) 32
4) 17
5) 33
6) 56
7) 33
8) 49
9) 6
10) − 9
11) 29
12) 9.8
13) 12
14) 62
15) 28
16) 10
17) 50
18) 18

Mixed Integer Computations

1) 14
2) − 42
3) 60
4) − 13
5) − 126
6) 24
7) 3
8) − 3
9) − 2
10) − 9
11) − 16
12) − 4
13) 28
14) − 49
15) 5
16) − 9
17) 12
18) 84
19) − 70
20) − 11

Absolute Value

1) 9
2) 18
3) −24
4) 3
5) 9
6) 2
7) 5
8) 6
9) 125
10) 24
11) 60
12) 66
13) 32
14) 63
15) 25
16) 11
17) 114
18) 24

Integers and Absolute Value

1) 4
2) 7
3) 8
4) 4
5) 5
6) 10
7) 1
8) 6
9) 8
10) 2
11) 1
12) 10
13) 3
14) 7
15) 5
16) 3
17) 9
18) 2
19) 4
20) 6
21) 9
22) 41
23) 133
24) 46
25) 44
26) 33
27) 15
28) 21
29) 23

Classifying Real Numbers Venn Diagram

1) 0: whole number, integer, rational number
2) − 5: integer, rational number
3) − 8.5: rational number
4) $\sqrt{4}$: natural number, whole number, integer, rational number
5) − 10: integer, rational number
6) 18 : natural number, whole number, integer, rational number
7) 6: natural number, whole number, integer, rational number
8) π: irrational number
9) $1\frac{2}{7}$: rational number
10) − 1: integer, rational number
11) $\sqrt{5}$: irrational number

Test Preparation Answers

1) Choice A is correct

Use PEMDAS (order of operation):

$8 - (-4) + (-15) \times 2 = 8 + 4 - 30 = -18$

2) The answer is 20.

Use PEMDAS (order of operation):

$4 + 8 \times (3) - [48] \div 6 = 4 + 24 - 8 = 20$

Chapter 4: Percent

Topics that you'll learn in this chapter:

- ✓ Percentage Calculations
- ✓ Converting Between Percent, Fractions, and Decimals
- ✓ Percent Problems
- ✓ Find What Percentage a Number Is of Another
- ✓ Find a Percentage of a Given Number
- ✓ Percent of Increase and Decrease

Percentage Calculations

> **Helpful Hints**
>
> - Use the following formula to find part, whole, or percent:
>   part = $\frac{percent}{100}$ × whole
>
> **Example:**
>
> $\frac{20}{100}$ × 100 = 20

✏️ **Calculate the percentages.**

1) 50% of 25

2) 80% of 15

3) 30% of 34

4) 70% of 45

5) 10% of 0

6) 80% of 22

7) 65% of 8

8) 78% of 54

9) 50% of 80

10) 20% of 10

11) 40% of 40

12) 90% of 0

13) 20% of 70

14) 55% of 60

15) 80% of 10

16) 20% of 880

17) 70% of 100

18) 80% of 90

✏️ **Solve.**

19) 50 is what percentage of 75?

20) What percentage of 100 is 70

21) Find what percentage of 60 is 35.

22) 40 is what percentage of 80?

Converting Between Percent, Fractions, and Decimals

Helpful Hints

– To a percent: Move the decimal point 2 places to the right and add the % symbol.

– Divide by 100 to convert a number from percent to decimal.

Examples:

30% = 0.3

0.24 = 24%

✎ *Converting fractions to decimals.*

1) $\dfrac{50}{100}$

2) $\dfrac{38}{100}$

3) $\dfrac{15}{100}$

4) $\dfrac{80}{100}$

5) $\dfrac{7}{100}$

6) $\dfrac{35}{100}$

7) $\dfrac{90}{100}$

8) $\dfrac{20}{100}$

9) $\dfrac{7}{100}$

✎ *Write each decimal as a percent.*

10) 0.5

11) 0.9

12) 0.002

13) 0.524

14) 0.1

15) 0.03

16) 3.63

17) 0.008

18) 4.78

Percent Problems

> **Helpful Hints**
>
> Base = Part ÷ Percent
> Part = Percent × Base
> Percent = Part ÷ Base
>
> **Example:**
>
> 2 is 10% of 20.
>
> 2 ÷ 0.10 = 20
>
> 2 = 0.10 × 20
>
> 0.10 = 2 ÷ 20

✎ Solve each problem.

1) 51 is 340% of what?

2) 93% of what number is 97?

3) 27% of 142 is what number?

4) What percent of 125 is 29.3?

5) 60 is what percent of 126?

6) 67 is 67% of what?

7) 67 is 13% of what?

8) 41% of 78 is what?

9) 1 is what percent of 52.6?

10) What is 59% of 14 m?

11) What is 90% of 130 inches?

12) 16 inches is 35% of what?

13) 90% of 54.4 hours is what?

14) What percent of 33.5 is 21?

15) Liam scored 22 out of 30 marks in Algebra, 35 out of 40 marks in science and 89 out of 100 marks in mathematics. In which subject his percentage of marks in best?

16) Ella require 50% to pass. If she gets 280 marks and falls short by 20 marks, what were the maximum marks she could have got?

Find What Percentage a Number Is of Another

> *Helpful Hints*
>
> PERCENT: the number with the percent sign (%).
> PART: the number with the word "is".
> WHOLE: the number with the word "of".
> — Divide the Part by the Base.
> — Convert the answer to percent.
>
> **Example:**
>
> 20 is what percent of 50?
>
> 20 ÷ 50 = 0.40 = 40%

Find the percentage of the numbers.

1) 5 is what percent of 90?

2) 15 is what percent of 75?

3) 20 is what percent of 400?

4) 18 is what percent of 90?

5) 3 is what percent of 15?

6) 8 is what percent of 80?

7) 11 is what percent of 55?

8) 9 is what percent of 90?

9) 2.5 is what percent of 10?

10) 5 is what percent of 25?

11) 60 is what percent of 20?

12) 12 is what percent of 48?

13) 14 is what percent of 28?

14) 8.2 is what percent of 32.8?

15) 1200 is what percent of 4,800?

16) 4,000 is what percent of 20,000?

17) 45 is what percent of 900?

18) 10 is what percent of 200?

19) 15 is what percent of 60?

20) 1.2 is what percent of 24?

Find a Percentage of a Given Number

Helpful Hints - Use following formula to find part, whole, or percent:

$$part = \frac{percent}{100} \times whole$$

Example:

$$\frac{50}{100} \times 50 = 25$$

Find a Percentage of a Given Number.

1) 90% of 50

2) 40% of 50

3) 10% of 0

4) 80% of 80

5) 60% of 40

6) 50% of 60

7) 30% of 20

8) 35% of 10

9) 10% of 80

10) 10% of 60

11) 100% 0f 50

12) 90% of 34

13) 80% of 42

14) 90% of 12

15) 20% of 56

16) 40% of 40

17) 40% of 6

18) 70% of 38

19) 30% of 3

20) 40% of 50

21) 100% of 8

Percent of Increase and Decrease

Helpful Hints

– To find the percentage increase:

New Number – Original Number

The result ÷ Original Number × 100

If your answer is a negative number, then this is a percentage decrease.

To calculate percentage decrease:

Original Number – New Number

The result ÷ Original Number × 100

Example:

From 84 miles to 24 miles = 71.43% decrease

Find each percent change to the nearest percent. Increase or decrease.

1) From 32 grams to 82 grams.

2) From 150 m to 45 m

3) From $438 to $443

4) From 256 ft to 140 ft

5) From 6469 ft to 7488 ft

6) From 36 inches to 90 inches

7) From 54 ft to 104 ft

8) From 84 miles to 24 miles

9) The population of a place in a particular year increased by 15%. Next year it decreased by 15%. Find the net increase or decrease percent in the initial population.

10) The salary of a doctor is increased by 40%. By what percent should the new salary be reduced in order to restore the original salary?

Test Preparation

1) Jason needs an 75% average in his writing class to pass. On his first 4 exams, he earned scores of 68%, 72%, 85%, and 90%. What is the minimum score Jason can earn on his fifth and final test to pass?

Write your answer in the box below.

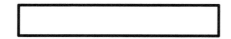

2) A shirt costing $200 is discounted 15%. Which of the following expressions can be used to find the selling price of the shirt?

   A. (200) (0.70)
   B. (200) − 200 (0.30)
   C. (200) (0.15) − (200) (0.15)
   D. (200) (0.85)

3) The price of a car was $20,000 in 2014 and $16,000 in 2015. What is the rate of depreciation of the price of the car per year?

   A. 15 %
   B. 20 %
   C. 25 %
   D. 30 %

4) The price of a laptop is decreased by 10% to $360. What is its original price?

   A. 320

   B. 380

   C. 400

   D. 450

5) A bank is offering 4.5% simple interest on a savings account. If you deposit $8,000, how much interest will you earn in five years?

   A. $360

   B. $720

   C. $1800

   D. $3600

6) There are 60 boys and 90 girls in a class. Of these students, 18 boys and 12 girls write left–handed. What percentage of the students in this class write left–handed?
   Write your answer in the box below.

7) 25 is What percent of 20?

   A. 20 %
   B. 25 %
   C. 125 %
   D. 150 %

8) A $40 shirt now selling for $28 is discounted by what percent?

   A. 20 %
   B. 30 %
   C. 40 %
   D. 60 %

9) From last year, the price of gasoline has increased from $1.25 per gallon to $1.75 per gallon. The new price is what percent of the original price?

   A. 72 %
   B. 120 %
   C. 140 %
   D. 160 %

10) Sophia purchased a sofa for $530.40. The sofa is regularly priced at $624. What was the percent discount Sophia received on the sofa?

A. 12%

B. 15%

C. 20%

D. 25%

11) 55 students took an exam and 11 of them failed. What percent of the students passed the exam?

A. 20 %
B. 40 %
C. 60 %
D. 80 %

12) Which of the following shows the numbers in descending order?

$$\frac{2}{3}, 0.68, 67\%, \frac{4}{5}$$

A. $67\%, 0.68, \frac{2}{3}, \frac{4}{5}$

B. $67\%, 0.68, \frac{4}{5}, \frac{2}{3}$

C. $\frac{4}{5}, 0.68, 67\%, \frac{2}{3}$

D. $\frac{2}{3}, 67\%, 0.68, \frac{4}{5}$

13) The price of a sofa is decreased by 25% to $420. What was its original price?

   A. $480
   B. $520
   C. $560
   D. $600

14) Mr. Jonson spent 44% of his income on rent last month. What fraction of his income did Mr. Jonson spend on rent?

   Write your answer in the box below.

   ☐

15) A bank is offering 3.5% simple interest on a savings account. If you deposit $12,000, how much interest will you earn in two years?

   A. $420
   B. $840
   C. $4200
   D. $8400

Answers of Worksheets – Chapter 4

Percentage Calculations

1) 12.5
2) 12
3) 10.2
4) 31.5
5) 0
6) 17.6
7) 5.2
8) 42.12
9) 40
10) 2
11) 16
12) 0
13) 14
14) 33
15) 8
16) 176
17) 70
18) 72
19) 67%
20) 70%
21) 58%
22) 50%

Converting Between Percent, Fractions, and Decimals

1) 0.5
2) 0.38
3) 0.15
4) 0.8
5) 0.07
6) 0.35
7) 0.9
8) 0.2
9) 0.07
10) 50%
11) 90%
12) 0.2%
13) 52.4%
14) 10%
15) 3%
16) 363%
17) 0.8%
18) 478%

Percent Problems

1) 15
2) 104.3
3) 38.34
4) 23.44%
5) 47.6%
6) 100
7) 515.4
8) 31.98
9) 1.9%
10) 8.3 m
11) 117 inches
12) 45.7 inches
13) 49 hours
14) 62.7%
15) Mathematics
16) 600

Find What Percentage a Number Is of Another

1) 45 is what percent of 90? 50 %
2) 15 is what percent of 75? 20 %
3) 20 is what percent of 400? 5 %
4) 18 is what percent of 90? 20 %
5) 3 is what percent of 15? 20 %
6) 8 is what percent of 80? 10 %
7) 11 is what percent of 55? 20 %
8) 9 is what percent of 90? 10 %
9) 2.5 is what percent of 10? 25 %
10) 5 is what percent of 25? 20 %
11) 60 is what percent of 20? 300 %
12) 12 is what percent of 48? 25 %
13) 14 is what percent of 28? 50 %
14) 8.2 is what percent of 32.8? 25 %
15) 1200 is what percent of 4,800? 25 %
16) 4,000 is what percent of 20,000? 20 %
17) 45 is what percent of 900? 5 %
18) 10 is what percent of 200? 5 %
19) 15 is what percent of 60? 25 %
20) 1.2 is what percent of 24? 5 %

Find a Percentage of a Given Number

1) 45
2) 20
3) 0
4) 64
5) 24
6) 30
7) 6
8) 3.5
9) 8
10) 6
11) 50
12) 30.6
13) 33.6
14) 10.8
15) 11.2
16) 16
17) 2.4
18) 26.6
19) 0.9
20) 20
21) 8

Percent of Increase and Decrease

1) 156.25% increase

2) 70% decrease

3) 1.142% increase

4) 45.31% decrease

5) 15.75% increase

6) 150% increase

7) 92.6% increase

8) 71.43% decrease

9) 2.25% decrease

10) $28\frac{4}{7}$ %

Test Preparation Answers

1) The answer is 60.

Jason needs an 75% average to pass for five exams. Therefore, the sum of 5 exams must be at least $5 \times 75 = 375$

The sum of 4 exams is:

$68 + 72 + 85 + 90 = 315$.

The minimum score Jason can earn on his fifth and final test to pass is:

$375 - 315 = 60$

2) Choice D is correct

To find the discount, multiply the number by (100% − rate of discount).

Therefore, for the first discount we get: $(200)(100\% - 15\%) = (200)(0.85) = 170$

For the next 15 % discount: $(200)(0.85)(0.85)$

3) Choice B is correct

Let x be the rate of depreciation.

If the price of a car is decreased by $4,000 to $16,000, then:

$x \% \ of \ \$20.000 = \$4.000 \Rightarrow \frac{x}{100} 20.000 = 4.000 \Rightarrow x = 4.000 \div 200 = 20$

8) Choice B is correct

Use the formula for Percent of Change

$$\frac{\text{New Value} - \text{Old Value}}{\text{Old Value}} \times 100\%$$

$\frac{28-40}{40} \times 100\% = -30\%$ (negative sign here means that the new price is less than old price).

9) Choice C is correct

Use percent formula:

$\text{part} = \frac{\text{percent}}{100} \times \text{whole}$

$1.75 = \frac{\text{percent}}{100} \times 1.25 \Rightarrow 1.75 = \frac{\text{percent} \times 1.25}{100} \Rightarrow 175 = \text{percent} \times 1.25 \Rightarrow$

$\text{percent} = \frac{175}{1.25} = 140$

10) Choice B is correct.

The question is this: 530.40 is what percent of 624?

Use percent formula:

$\text{part} = \frac{\text{percent}}{100} \times \text{whole}$

$530.40 = \frac{\text{percent}}{100} \times 624 \Rightarrow 530.40 = \frac{\text{percent} \times 624}{100} \Rightarrow 53040 = \text{percent} \times 624 \Rightarrow$

$\text{percent} = \frac{53040}{624} = 85$

530.40 is 85 % of 624. Therefore, the discount is: 100% − 85% = 15%

11) Choice D is correct

The failing rate is 11 out of 55 = $\frac{11}{55}$

Change the fraction to percent:

$\frac{11}{55} \times 100\% = 20\%$

20 percent of students failed. Therefore, 80 percent of students passed the exam.

4) Choice C is correct

Let x be the original price.

If the price of a laptop is decreased by 10% to $360, then:

$90\% \ of \ x = 360 \Rightarrow 0.90x = 360 \Rightarrow x = 360 \div 0.90 = 400$

5) Choice C is correct

Use simple interest formula:

$I = prt$

(I = interest, p = principal, r = rate, t = time)

$$I = (8000)(0.045)(5) = 1800$$

6) The answer is 20%.

The whole number of students = 60 boys + 90 girls = 150

The amount of students that write left-handed = 18 boys + 12 girls = 30

Let x be the percentage of the students that write left-handed.

$x \ \% \ of \ total \ students = \text{left} - \text{handed students} \Rightarrow x \ \% \ 150 = 30 \Rightarrow x = 3000 \div 150 = 20\%$

7) Choice C is correct

Use percent formula:

$\text{part} = \frac{\text{percent}}{100} \times \text{whole}$

$25 = \frac{\text{percent}}{100} \times 20 \Rightarrow 25 = \frac{\text{percent} \times 20}{100} \Rightarrow 25 = \frac{\text{percent} \times 2}{10}$, multiply both sides by 10.

250 = percent $\times$ 2, divide both sides by 2.

125 = percent

12) Choice D is correct

Change the numbers to decimal and then compare.

$\frac{2}{3} = 0.666...$

0.68

$67\% = 0.67$

$\frac{4}{5} = 0.80$

Therefore

$\frac{2}{3} < 67\% < 0.68 < \frac{4}{5}$

13) Choice C is correct.

Let x be the original price.

If the price of the sofa is decreased by 25% to $420, then: $75\ \%\ of\ x = 420 \Rightarrow 0.75x = 420 \Rightarrow x = 420 \div 0.75 = 560$

14) The answer is $\frac{44}{100}$.

$44\% = \frac{44}{100}$

15) Choice B is correct

Use simple interest formula:

$I = prt$

(I = interest, p = principal, r = rate, t = time)

$$I = (12000)(0.035)(2) = 840$$

Chapter 5: Algebraic Expressions

Topics that you'll learn in this chapter:

- ✓ Expressions and Variables
- ✓ Simplifying Variable Expressions
- ✓ Translate Phrases into an Algebraic Statement
- ✓ The Distributive Property
- ✓ Evaluating One Variable
- ✓ Evaluating Two Variables
- ✓ Combining like Terms

Expressions and Variables

Helpful Hints

A variable is a letter that represents unknown numbers. A variable can be used in the same manner as all other numbers:

Addition	$2 + a$	2 plus a
Subtraction	$y - 3$	y minus 3
Division	$\dfrac{4}{x}$	4 divided by x
Multiplication	$5a$	5 times a

✎ Simplify each expression.

1) $x + 5x$,
   use $x = 5$

2) $8(-3x + 9) + 6$,
   use $x = 6$

3) $10x - 2x + 6 - 5$,
   use $x = 5$

4) $2x - 3x - 9$,
   use $x = 7$

5) $(-6)(-2x - 4y)$,
   use $x = 1, y = 3$

6) $8x + 2 + 4y$,
   use $x = 9, y = 2$

7) $(-6)(-8x - 9y)$,
   use $x = 5, y = 5$

8) $6x + 5y$,
   use $x = 7, y = 4$

✎ Simplify each expression.

9) $5(-4 + 2x)$

10) $-3 - 5x - 6x + 9$

11) $6x - 3x - 8 + 10$

12) $(-8)(6x - 4) + 12$

13) $9(7x + 4) + 6x$

14) $(-9)(-5x + 2)$

Simplifying Variable Expressions

Helpful Hints

– Combine "like" terms. (values with same variable and same power)

– Use distributive property if necessary.

Distributive Property:

$a(b + c) = ab + ac$

Example:

$2x + 2(1 - 5x) =$

$2x + 2 - 10x = -8x + 2$

✏ Simplify each expression.

1) $-2 - x^2 - 6x^2$

2) $3 + 10x^2 + 2$

3) $8x^2 + 6x + 7x^2$

4) $5x^2 - 12x^2 + 8x$

5) $2x^2 - 2x - x$

6) $(-6)(8x - 4)$

7) $4x + 6(2 - 5x)$

8) $10x + 8(10x - 6)$

9) $9(-2x - 6) - 5$

10) $3(x + 9)$

11) $7x + 3 - 3x$

12) $2.5x^2 \times (-8x)$

✏ Simplify.

13) $-2(4 - 6x) - 3x$, $x = 1$

14) $2x + 8x$, $x = 2$

15) $9 - 2x + 5x + 2$, $x = 5$

16) $5(3x + 7)$, $x = 3$

17) $2(3 - 2x) - 4$, $x = 6$

18) $5x + 3x - 8$, $x = 3$

19) $x - 7x$, $x = 8$

20) $5(-2 - 9x)$, $x = 4$

Translate Phrases into an Algebraic Statement

Helpful Hints

Translating key words and phrases into algebraic expressions:

Addition: plus, more than, the sum of, etc.

Subtraction: minus, less than, decreased, etc.

Multiplication: times, product, multiplied, etc.

Division: quotient, divided, ratio, etc.

Example:

eight more than a number is 20

$8 + x = 20$

✎ *Write an algebraic expression for each phrase.*

1) A number increased by forty–two.

2) The sum of fifteen and a number

3) The difference between fifty–six and a number.

4) The quotient of thirty and a number.

5) Twice a number decreased by 25.

6) Four times the sum of a number and − 12.

7) A number divided by − 20.

8) The quotient of 60 and the product of a number and − 5.

9) Ten subtracted from a number.

10) The difference of six and a number.

The Distributive Property

> **Helpful Hints**
>
> Distributive Property:
>
> $a(b + c) = ab + ac$
>
> Example:
>
> $3(4 + 3x)$
>
> $= 12 + 9x$

✎ Use the distributive property to simply each expression.

1) $-(-2 - 5x)$

2) $(-6x + 2)(-1)$

3) $(-5)(x - 2)$

4) $-(7 - 3x)$

5) $8(8 + 2x)$

6) $2(12 + 2x)$

7) $(-6x + 8)4$

8) $(3 - 6x)(-7)$

9) $(-12)(2x + 1)$

10) $(8 - 2x)9$

11) $(-2x)(-1 + 9x) - 4x(4 + 5x)$

12) $3(-5x - 3) + 4(6 - 3x)$

13) $(-2)(x + 4) - (2 + 3x)$

14) $(-4)(3x - 2) + 6(x + 1)$

15) $(-5)(4x - 1) + 4(x + 2)$

16) $(-3)(x + 4) - (2 + 3x)$

Evaluating One Variable

Helpful Hints
- To evaluate one variable expression, find the variable and substitute a number for that variable.
- Perform the arithmetic operations.

Example:

$4x + 8, x = 6$

$4(6) + 8 = 24 + 8 = 32$

✎ *Simplify each algebraic expression.*

1) $9 - x$, $x = 3$

2) $x + 2$, $x = 5$

3) $3x + 7$, $x = 6$

4) $x + (-5)$, $x = -2$

5) $3x + 6$, $x = 4$

6) $4x + 6$, $x = -1$

7) $10 + 2x - 6$, $x = 3$

8) $10 - 3x$, $x = 8$

9) $\frac{20}{x} - 3$, $x = 5$

10) $(-3) + \frac{x}{4} + 2x$, $x = 16$

11) $(-2) + \frac{x}{7}$, $x = 21$

12) $(-\frac{14}{x}) - 9 + 4x$, $x = 2$

13) $(-\frac{6}{x}) - 9 + 2x$, $x = 3$

14) $(-2) + \frac{x}{8}$, $x = 16$

15) $8(5x - 12)$, $x = -2$

Evaluating Two Variables

Helpful Hints

To evaluate an algebraic expression, substitute a number for each variable and perform the arithmetic operations.

Example:

$2x + 4y - 3 + 2,$

$x = 5, y = 3$

$2(5) + 4(3) - 3 + 2$
$= 10 + 12 - 3 + 2$
$= 21$

✎ Simplify each algebraic expression.

1) $2x + 4y - 3 + 2,$
   $x = 5, y = 3$

2) $(-\frac{12}{x}) + 1 + 5y,$
   $x = 6, y = 8$

3) $(-4)(-2a - 2b),$
   $a = 5, b = 3$

4) $10 + 3x + 7 - 2y,$
   $x = 7, y = 6$

5) $9x + 2 - 4y,$
   $x = 7, y = 5$

6) $6 + 3(-2x - 3y),$
   $x = 9, y = 7$

7) $12x + y,$
   $x = 4, y = 8$

8) $x \times 4 \div y,$
   $x = 3, y = 2$

9) $2x + 14 + 4y,$
   $x = 6, y = 8$

10) $4a - (5 - b),$
    $a = 4, b = 6$

Combining like Terms

Helpful Hints
- Terms are separated by "+" and "−" signs.
- Like terms are terms with same variables and same powers.
- Be sure to use the "+" or "−" that is in front of the coefficient.

Example:

$22x + 6 + 2x =$

$24x + 6$

✍ *Simplify each expression.*

1) $5 + 2x − 8$

2) $(− 2x + 6)\,2$

3) $7 + 3x + 6x − 4$

4) $(− 4) − (3)(5x + 8)$

5) $9x − 7x − 5$

6) $x − 12x$

7) $7(3x + 6) + 2x$

8) $(− 11x) − 10x$

9) $3x − 12 − 5x$

10) $13 + 4x − 5$

11) $(− 22x) + 8x$

12) $2(4 + 3x) − 7x$

13) $(− 4x) − (6 − 14x)$

14) $5(6x − 1) + 12x$

15) $22x + 6 + 2x$

16) $(− 13x) − 14x$

17) $(− 6x) − 9 + 15x$

18) $(− 6x) + 7x$

19) $(− 5x) + 12 + 7x$

20) $(− 3x) − 9 + 15x$

21) $20x − 19x$

Test Preparation

1) Which expression is equivalent to $38x$?

   A. $(x \times 30) \times 8$
   B. $(x \times 30) + 8$
   C. $(x \times 30) + (x \times 8)$
   D. $(x \times 3) + 8$

Answers of Worksheets – Chapter 5

Expressions and Variables

1) 30
2) −66
3) 41
4) −16
5) 84
6) 82
7) 510
8) 62
9) 10x − 20
10) 6 − 11x
11) 3x + 2
12) 44 − 48x
13) 69x + 36
14) 45x − 18

Simplifying Variable Expressions

1) $-7x^2 - 2$
2) $10x^2 + 5$
3) $15x^2 + 6x$
4) $-7x^2 + 8x$
5) $2x^2 - 3x$
6) $-48x + 24$
7) $-26x + 12$
8) $90x - 48$
9) $-18x - 59$
10) $3x + 27$
11) $4x + 3$
12) $-20x^3$
13) 1
14) 20
15) 26
16) 80
17) −22
18) 16
19) −48
20) −190

Translate Phrases into an Algebraic Statement

1) $x + 42$
2) $15 + x$
3) $56 - x$
4) $30/x$
5) $2x - 25$
6) $4(x + (-12))$
7) $\dfrac{x}{-20}$
8) $\dfrac{60}{-5x}$
9) $x - 10$
10) $6 - x$

The Distributive Property

1) $5x + 2$
2) $6x - 2$
3) $-5x + 10$
4) $3x - 7$
5) $16x + 64$
6) $4x + 24$
7) $-24x + 32$
8) $42x - 21$
9) $-24x - 12$
10) $-18x + 72$
11) $-38x^2 - 14x$
12) $-27x + 15$
13) $-5x - 10$
14) $-6x + 14$
15) $-16x + 13$
16) $-6x - 14$

Evaluating One Variable

1) 6
2) 7
3) 25
4) −7
5) 18
6) 2
7) 10
8) −14
9) 1
10) 33
11) 1
12) −8
13) −5
14) 0
15) −176

Evaluating Two Variables

1) 21
2) 39
3) 64
4) 26
5) 45
6) −111
7) 56
8) 6
9) 58
10) 17

Combining like Terms

1) $2x - 3$
2) $-4x + 12$
3) $9x + 3$
4) $-15x - 28$
5) $2x - 5$
6) $-11x$
7) $23x + 42$
8) $-21x$
9) $-2x - 12$
10) $4x + 8$
11) $-14x$
12) $-x + 8$
13) $10x - 6$
14) $42x - 5$
15) $24x + 6$
16) $-27x$
17) $9x - 9$
18) x
19) $2x + 12$
20) $12x - 9$
21) x

Test Preparation Answers

1) Choice C is correct.

Let scan alternatives on by one.

A. $(30x) \times 8 = 240x$

B. $(30x) + 8 = 30x + 8$

C. $(30x) + (8x) = 38x$

D. $(3x) + 8 = 3x + 8$

Chapter 6: Equations

Topics that you'll learn in this chapter:

- ✓ One–Step Equations
- ✓ One–Step Equation Word Problems
- ✓ Two–Step Equations
- ✓ Two–Step Equation Word Problems
- ✓ Multi–Step Equations

One–Step Equations

Helpful Hints

- The values of two expressions on both sides of an equation are equal.
$$ax + b = c$$
- You only need to perform one Math operation in order to solve the equation.

Example:

$$-8x = 16$$

$$x = -2$$

✎ Solve each equation.

1) $x + 3 = 17$

2) $22 = (-8) + x$

3) $3x = (-30)$

4) $(-36) = (-6x)$

5) $(-6) = 4 + x$

6) $2 + x = (-2)$

7) $20x = (-220)$

8) $18 = x + 5$

9) $(-23) + x = (-19)$

10) $5x = (-45)$

11) $x - 12 = (-25)$

12) $x - 3 = (-12)$

13) $(-35) = x - 27$

14) $8 = 2x$

15) $(-6x) = 36$

16) $(-55) = (-5x)$

17) $x - 30 = 20$

18) $8x = 32$

19) $36 = (-4x)$

20) $4x = 68$

21) $30x = 300$

One–Step Equation Word Problems

> *Helpful Hints*
> – Define the variable.
> – Translate key words and phrases into math equation.
> – Isolate the variable and solve the equation.

✍ *Solve.*

1) How many boxes of envelopes can you buy with $18 if one box costs $3?

2) After paying $6.25 for a salad, Ella has $45.56. How much money did she have before buying the salad?

3) How many packages of diapers can you buy with $50 if one package costs $5?

4) Last week James ran 20 miles more than Michael. James ran 56 miles. How many miles did Michael run?

5) Last Friday Jacob had $32.52. Over the weekend he received some money for cleaning the attic. He now has $44. How much money did he receive?

6) After paying $10.12 for a sandwich, Amelia has $35.50. How much money did she have before buying the sandwich?

Two–Step Equations

Helpful Hints

– You only need to perform two math operations (add, subtract, multiply, or divide) to solve the equation.

– Simplify using the inverse of addition or subtraction.

– Simplify further by using the inverse of multiplication or division.

Example:

$-2(x-1) = 42$

$(x-1) = -21$

$x = -20$

✎ Solve each equation.

1) $5(8 + x) = 20$

2) $(-7)(x - 9) = 42$

3) $(-12)(2x - 3) = (-12)$

4) $6(1 + x) = 12$

5) $12(2x + 4) = 60$

6) $7(3x + 2) = 42$

7) $8(14 + 2x) = (-34)$

8) $(-15)(2x - 4) = 48$

9) $3(x + 5) = 12$

10) $\dfrac{3x - 12}{6} = 4$

11) $(-12) = \dfrac{x + 15}{6}$

12) $110 = (-5)(2x - 6)$

13) $\dfrac{x}{8} - 12 = 4$

14) $20 = 12 + \dfrac{x}{4}$

15) $\dfrac{-24 + x}{6} = (-12)$

16) $(-4)(5 + 2x) = (-100)$

17) $(-12x) + 20 = 32$

18) $\dfrac{-2 + 6x}{4} = (-8)$

19) $\dfrac{x + 6}{5} = (-5)$

20) $(-9) + \dfrac{x}{4} = (-15)$

Two–Step Equation Word Problems

> *Helpful Hints*
> – Translate the word problem into equations with variables.
> – Solve the equations to find the solutions to the word problems.

✎ Solve.

1) The sum of three consecutive even numbers is 48. What is the smallest of these numbers?

2) How old am I if 400 reduced by 2 times my age is 244?

3) For a field trip, 4 students rode in cars and the rest filled nine buses. How many students were in each bus if 472 students were on the trip?

4) The sum of three consecutive numbers is 72. What is the smallest of these numbers?

5) 331 students went on a field trip. Six buses were filled, and 7 students traveled in cars. How many students were in each bus?

6) You bought a magazine for $5 and four erasers. You spent a total of $25. How much did each eraser cost?

Multi–Step Equations

Helpful Hints

– Combine "like" terms on one side.

– Bring variables to one side by adding or subtracting.

– Simplify using the inverse of addition or subtraction.

– Simplify further by using the inverse of multiplication or division.

Example:

$3x + 15 = -2x + 5$

Add 2x both sides

$5x + 15 = +5$

Subtract 15 both sides

$5x = -10$

Divide by 5 both sides

$x = -2$

✎ Solve each equation.

1) $-(2 - 2x) = 10$

2) $-12 = -(2x + 8)$

3) $3x + 15 = (-2x) + 5$

4) $-28 = (-2x) - 12x$

5) $2(1 + 2x) + 2x = -118$

6) $3x - 18 = 22 + x - 3 + x$

7) $12 - 2x = (-32) - x + x$

8) $7 - 3x - 3x = 3 - 3x$

9) $6 + 10x + 3x = (-30) + 4x$

10) $(-3x) - 8(-1 + 5x) = 352$

11) $24 = (-4x) - 8 + 8$

12) $9 = 2x - 7 + 6x$

13) $6(1 + 6x) = 294$

14) $-10 = (-4x) - 6x$

15) $4x - 2 = (-7) + 5x$

16) $5x - 14 = 8x + 4$

17) $40 = -(4x - 8)$

18) $(-18) - 6x = 6(1 + 3x)$

19) $x - 5 = -2(6 + 3x)$

20) $6 = 1 - 2x + 5$

Test Preparation

1) What is the value of x in the following equation?

$$x + \frac{1}{6} = \frac{1}{3}$$

A. 6

B. $\frac{1}{2}$

C. $\frac{1}{6}$

D. $\frac{1}{4}$

2) The area of a rectangle is x square feet and its length is 9 feet. Which equation represents y, the width of the rectangle in feet?

A. $y = \frac{x}{9}$

B. $y = \frac{9}{x}$

C. $y = 9x$

D. $y = 9 + x$

3) An angle is equal to one fifth of its supplement. What is the measure of that angle?

   A. 20
   B. 30
   C. 45
   D. 60

4) In five successive hours, a car travels 40 km, 45 km, 50 km, 35 km and 55 km. In the next five hours, it travels with an average speed of 50 km per hour. Find the total distance the car traveled in 10 hours.

   A. 425 km
   B. 450 km
   C. 475 km
   D. 500 km

5) In a triangle ABC the measure of angle ACB is 75° and the measure of angle CAB is 45°. What is the measure of angle ABC?

   Write your answer in the box below.

   ☐

6) Which expression is equivalent to $40 \div (4 + x)$?

   A. $40 \div 4 + 40 \div x$
   B. $(4 + x) \div 40$
   C. $(x + 4) + 40$
   D. $40 \div (x + 4)$

7) If 40 % of a number is 4, what is the number?

   A. 4
   B. 8
   C. 10
   D. 12

8) Jason is 9 miles ahead of Joe running at 5.5 miles per hour and Joe is running at the speed of 7 miles per hour. How long does it take Joe to catch Jason?

   A. 3 hours
   B. 4 hours
   C. 6 hours
   D. 8 hours

9) What is the equivalent temperature of 104°F in Celsius?

$$C = \frac{5}{9}(F - 32)$$

A. 32

B. 40

C. 48

D. 52

10) If 150 % of a number is 75, then what is the 90 % of that number?

A. 45

B. 50

C. 70

D. 85

11) If $x = -8$, which equation is true?

A. $x(2x - 4) = 120$

B. $8(4 - x) = 96$

C. $2(4x + 6) = 79$

D. $6x - 2 = -46$

Answers of Worksheets – Chapter 6

One–Step Equations

1) 14	8) 13	15) − 6
2) 30	9) 4	16) 11
3) − 10	10) − 9	17) 50
4) 6	11) − 13	18) 4
5) − 10	12) − 9	19) − 9
6) − 4	13) − 8	20) 17
7) − 11	14) 4	21) 10

One–Step Equation Word Problems

1) 6	3) 10	5) 11.48
2) $51.81	4) 36	6) 45.62

Two–Step Equations

1) − 4	8) $\frac{2}{5}$	15) − 48
2) 3	9) − 1	16) 10
3) 2	10) 12	17) − 1
4) 1	11) − 87	18) − 5
5) 0.5	12) − 8	19) − 31
6) $\frac{4}{3}$	13) 128	20) − 24
7) $-\frac{73}{8}$	14) 32	

Two–Step Equation Word Problems

1) 14	3) 52	5) 54
2) 78	4) 23	6) $4

Multi–Step Equations

1) 6
2) 2
3) −2
4) 2
5) −20
6) 37
7) 22
8) $\frac{4}{3}$
9) −4
10) −8
11) −6
12) 2
13) 8
14) 1
15) 5
16) −6
17) −8
18) −1
19) −1
20) 0

Test Preparation Answers

1) The answer is C.

Subtract the numerators and find x.

$x = \frac{1}{3} - \frac{1}{6} \Rightarrow x = \frac{2-1}{6} \Rightarrow x = \frac{1}{6}$

2) Choice A is correct

To find the area of rectangle = width multiply length

Therefore; $x = 9 \times y$

Then find y : $y = \frac{x}{9}$

3) Choice B is correct

The sum of supplement angles is 180. Let x be that angle. Therefore,

$x + 5x = 180$

$6x = 180$, divide both sides by 6: $x = 30$

4) Choice C is correct

Add the first 5 numbers. $40 + 45 + 50 + 35 + 55 = 225$

To find the distance traveled in the next 5 hours, multiply the average by number of hours.

Distance = Average × Rate = $50 \times 5 = 250$

Add both numbers.

$250 + 225 = 475$

5) **The answer is 60.**

The whole angles in every triangle are: 180° and Let x be the number of new angle so:

$180 = 75 + 45 + x \Rightarrow x = 60°$

6) **Choice A is correct.**

7) **Choice C is correct**

Let x be the number. Write the equation and solve for x.

$40\% \ of \ x = 4 \Rightarrow 0.40 \ x = 4 \Rightarrow x = 4 \div 0.40 = 10$

8) **Choice C is correct**

The distance between Jason and Joe is 9 miles. Jason running at 5.5 miles per hour and Joe is running at the speed of 7 miles per hour. Therefore, every hour the distance is 1.5 miles less. $9 \div 1.5 = 6$

9) **Choice B is correct**

Plug in 104 for F and then solve for C.

$C = \frac{5}{9}(F - 32) \Rightarrow C = \frac{5}{9}(104 - 32) \Rightarrow C = \frac{5}{9}(72) = 40$

10) Choice A is correct

First, find the number.

Let x be the number. Write the equation and solve for x.

150 % of a number is 75, then:

$1.5 \times x = 75 \Rightarrow x = 75 \div 1.5 = 50$

90 % of 50 is:

0.9 × 50 = 45

11) Choice B is correct.

$8(4 - x) = 96 \Rightarrow 8(4 - (-8)) = 96$

Chapter 7: Proportions and Ratios

Topics that you'll learn in this chapter:

- ✓ Writing Ratios
- ✓ Simplifying Ratios
- ✓ Proportional Ratios
- ✓ Create a Proportion
- ✓ Similar Figures
- ✓ Similar Figure Word Problems
- ✓ Ratio and Rates Word Problems

Writing Ratios

> **Helpful Hints**
>
> – A ratio is a comparison of two numbers. Ratio can be written as a division.
>
> **Example:**
>
> $3 : 5$, or $\dfrac{3}{5}$

✎ **Express each ratio as a rate and unite rate.**

1) 120 miles on 4 gallons of gas.

2) 24 dollars for 6 books.

3) 200 miles on 14 gallons of gas

4) 24 inches of snow in 8 hours

✎ **Express each ratio as a fraction in the simplest form.**

5) 3 feet out of 30 feet

6) 18 cakes out of 42 cakes

7) 16 dimes t0 24 dimes

8) 12 dimes out of 48 coins

9) 14 cups to 84 cups

10) 45 gallons to 65 gallons

11) 10 miles out of 40 miles

12) 22 blue cars out of 55 cars

13) 32 pennies to 300 pennies

14) 24 beetles out of 86 insects

Proportional Ratios

Helpful Hints

– A proportion means that two ratios are equal. It can be written in two ways:

$\dfrac{a}{b} = \dfrac{c}{d}$, a : b = c : d

Example:

$\dfrac{9}{3} = \dfrac{6}{d}$

d = 2

Solve each proportion.

1) $\dfrac{3}{6} = \dfrac{8}{d}$

2) $\dfrac{k}{5} = \dfrac{12}{15}$

3) $\dfrac{30}{5} = \dfrac{12}{x}$

4) $\dfrac{x}{2} = \dfrac{1}{8}$

5) $\dfrac{d}{3} = \dfrac{2}{6}$

6) $\dfrac{27}{7} = \dfrac{30}{x}$

7) $\dfrac{8}{5} = \dfrac{k}{15}$

8) $\dfrac{60}{20} = \dfrac{3}{d}$

9) $\dfrac{x}{3} = \dfrac{12}{18}$

10) $\dfrac{25}{5} = \dfrac{x}{8}$

11) $\dfrac{12}{x} = \dfrac{4}{2}$

12) $\dfrac{x}{4} = \dfrac{18}{2}$

13) $\dfrac{80}{10} = \dfrac{k}{10}$

14) $\dfrac{12}{6} = \dfrac{6}{d}$

15) $\dfrac{x}{4} = \dfrac{30}{5}$

16) $\dfrac{9}{5} = \dfrac{k}{5}$

17) $\dfrac{45}{15} = \dfrac{15}{d}$

18) $\dfrac{60}{x} = \dfrac{10}{3}$

19) $\dfrac{d}{3} = \dfrac{14}{6}$

20) $\dfrac{k}{4} = \dfrac{4}{2}$

21) $\dfrac{4}{2} = \dfrac{x}{7}$

Simplifying Ratios

Helpful Hints

− You can calculate equivalent ratios by multiplying or dividing both sides of the ratio by the same number.

Examples:

3 : 6 = 1 : 2

4 : 9 = 8 : 18

✎ *Reduce each ratio.*

1) 21 : 49

2) 20 : 40

3) 10 : 50

4) 14 : 18

5) 45 : 27

6) 49 : 21

7) 100 : 10

8) 12 : 8

9) 35 : 45

10) 8 : 20

11) 25 : 35

12) 21 : 27

13) 52 : 82

14) 12 : 36

15) 24 : 3

16) 15 : 30

17) 3 : 36

18) 8 : 16

19) 6 : 100

20) 2 : 20

21) 10 : 60

22) 14 : 63

23) 68 : 80

24) 8 : 80

Create a Proportion

Helpful Hints

– A proportion contains 2 equal fractions! A proportion simply means that two fractions are equal.

Example:

2, 4, 8, 16

$$\frac{2}{4} = \frac{8}{16}$$

✏️ *Create proportion from the given set of numbers.*

1) 1, 6, 2, 3

2) 12, 144, 1, 12

3) 16, 4, 8, 2

4) 9, 5, 27, 15

5) 7, 10, 60, 42

6) 8, 7, 24, 21

7) 10, 5, 8, 4

8) 3, 12, 8, 2

9) 2, 2, 1, 4

10) 3, 6, 7, 14

11) 2, 6, 5, 15

12) 7, 2, 14, 4

Similar Figures

Helpful Hints	– Two or more figures are similar if the corresponding angles are equal, and the corresponding sides are in proportion.	**Example:** 3–4–5 triangle is similar to a 6–8–10 triangle

✍ *Each pair of figures is similar. Find the missing side.*

1)

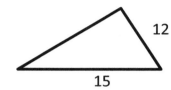 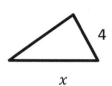

2)

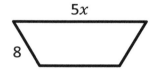 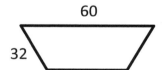

3)

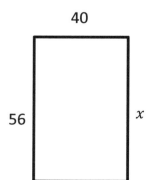

Similar Figure Word Problems

Helpful Hints

To solve a similarity word problem, create a proportion and use cross multiplication method!

Example:

$$\frac{x}{4} = \frac{8}{16}$$

$$16x = 4 \times 8$$

$$x = 2$$

✏️ *Answer each question and round your answer to the nearest whole number.*

1) If a 42.9 ft tall flagpole casts a 253.1 ft long shadow, then how long is the shadow that a 6.2 ft tall woman casts?

2) A model igloo has a scale of 1 in : 2 ft. If the real igloo is 10 ft wide, then how wide is the model igloo?

3) If a 18 ft tall tree casts a 9 ft long shadow, then how tall is an adult giraffe that casts a 7 ft shadow?

4) Find the distance between San Joe and Mount Pleasant if they are 2 cm apart on a map with a scale of 1 cm : 9 km.

5) A telephone booth that is 8 ft tall casts a shadow that is 4 ft long. Find the height of a lawn ornament that casts a 2 ft shadow.

Ratio and Rates Word Problems

Helpful *Hints*	To solve a ratio or a rate word problem, create a proportion and use cross multiplication method!	Example: $\frac{x}{4} = \frac{8}{16}$ $16x = 4 \times 8$ $x = 2$

 Solve.

1) In a party, 10 soft drinks are required for every 12 guests. If there are 252 guests, how many soft drink is required?

2) In Jack's class, 18 of the students are tall and 10 are short. In Michael's class 54 students are tall and 30 students are short. Which class has a higher ratio of tall to short students?

3) Are these ratios equivalent?
   12 cards to 72 animals 11 marbles to 66 marbles

4) The price of 3 apples at the Quick Market is $1.44. The price of 5 of the same apples at Walmart is $2.50. Which place is the better buy?

5) The bakers at a Bakery can make 160 bagels in 4 hours. How many bagels can they bake in 16 hours? What is that rate per hour?

6) You can buy 5 cans of green beans at a supermarket for $3.40. How much does it cost to buy 35 cans of green beans?

Test Preparation

1) The ratio of boys and girls in a class is 4:7. If there are 44 students in the class, how many more boys should be enrolled to make the ratio 1:1?

   A. 8
   B. 10
   C. 12
   D. 14

2) In a party, 6 soft drinks are required for every 9 guests. If there are 171 guests, how many soft drink is required?

   A. 9
   B. 27
   C. 114
   D. 171

3) Peter traveled 150 km in 6 hours and Jason traveled 180 km in 4 hours. What is the ratio of the average speed of Peter to average speed of Jason?

   A. 3 : 2
   B. 2 : 3
   C. 5 : 9
   D. 5 : 6

4) How long does a 420–miles trip take moving at 50 miles per hour (mph)?

   A. 4 hours
   B. 6 hours and 24 minutes
   C. 8 hours and 24 minutes
   D. 8 hours and 30 minutes

5) The ratio of boys to girls in a school is 3:4. If there are 350 students in a school, how many boys are in the school.

   Write your answer in the box below.

Answers of Worksheets – Chapter 7

Writing Ratios

1) $\frac{120\ miles}{4\ gallons}$, 30 miles per gallon

2) $\frac{24\ dollars}{6\ books}$, 4.00 dollars per book

3) $\frac{200\ miles}{14\ gallons}$, 14.29 miles per gallon

4) $\frac{24"\ of\ snow}{8\ hours}$, 3 inches of snow per hour

5) $\frac{1}{10}$
6) $\frac{3}{7}$
7) $\frac{2}{3}$
8) $\frac{1}{4}$

9) $\frac{1}{6}$
10) $\frac{9}{13}$
11) $\frac{1}{4}$
12) $\frac{2}{5}$

13) $\frac{8}{75}$
14) $\frac{12}{43}$

Simplifying Ratios

1) 3 : 7
2) 1 : 2
3) 1 : 5
4) 7 : 9
5) 5 : 3
6) 7 : 3
7) 10 : 1
8) 3 : 2

9) 7 : 9
10) 2 : 5
11) 5 : 7
12) 7 : 9
13) 26 : 41
14) 1 : 3
15) 8 : 1
16) 1 : 2

17) 1 : 12
18) 1 : 2
19) 3 : 50
20) 1 : 10
21) 1 : 6
22) 2 : 9
23) 17 : 20
24) 1 : 10

Proportional Ratios

1) 16
2) 4
3) 2
4) 0.25

5) 1
6) 7.78
7) 24
8) 1

9) 2
10) 40
11) 6
12) 36

13) 80	16) 9	19) 7
14) 3	17) 5	20) 8
15) 24	18) 18	21) 14

Create a Proportion

1) 1 : 3 = 2 : 6	5) 7 : 42, 10 : 60	9) 4 : 2 = 2 : 1
2) 12 : 144 = 1 : 12	6) 7 : 21 = 8 : 24	10) 7 : 3 = 14 : 6
3) 2 : 4 = 8 : 16	7) 8 : 10 = 4 : 5	11) 5 : 2 = 15 : 6
4) 5 : 15 = 9 : 27	8) 2 : 3 = 8 : 12	12) 7 : 2 = 14 : 4

Similar Figures

1) 5	2) 3	3) 56

Similar Figure Word Problems

1) 36.6 ft	3) 14 ft	5) 4 ft
2) 5 in	4) 18 km	

Ratio and Rates Word Problems

1) 210
2) The ratio for both class is equal to 9 to 5.
3) Yes! Both ratios are 1 to 6
4) The price at the Quick Market is a better buy.
5) 640, the rate is 40 per hour.
6) $23.80

Test Preparation Answers

1) Choice C is correct

The ratio of boy to girls is 4:7. Therefore, there are 4 boys out of 11 students. To find the answer, first divide the total number of students by 11, then multiply the result by 4.

44 ÷ 11 = 4 ⟹ 4 × 4 = 16

There are 16 boys and 28 (44 − 16) girls. So, 12 more boys should be enrolled to make the ratio 1:1

2) Choice C is correct

Let x be the number of soft drinks for 171 guests. It's needed to have a proportional ratio to find x.

$$\frac{6 \text{ soft drinks}}{9 \text{ guests}} = \frac{x}{171 \text{ guests}}$$

$$x = \frac{171 \times 6}{9} \Rightarrow x = 114$$

3) Choice C is correct

Speed = $\frac{\text{The amount of Km}}{\text{The amount of hours}}$

Peter's speed = $\frac{150}{6}$ = 25

Jason's speed = $\frac{180}{4}$ = 45

$\frac{\text{The average speed of peter}}{\text{The average speed of Jason}} = \frac{25}{45}$ and after simplification we have: $\frac{5}{9}$

4) Choice C is correct

Use distance formula:

Distance = Rate × time $\Rightarrow$ 420 = 50 × T, divide both sides by 50. 420 / 50 = T $\Rightarrow$ T = 8.4 hours.

Change hours to minutes for the decimal part. 0.4 hours = 0.4 × 60 = 24 minutes.

5) The answer is 150.

The ratio of boy to girls is 3:4. Therefore, there are 3 boys out of 7 students. To find the answer, first divide the total number of students by 7, then multiply the result by 3.

350 ÷ 7 = 50 $\Rightarrow$ 50 × 3 = 150

Chapter 8: Inequalities

Topics that you'll learn in this chapter:

- ✓ Graphing Single– Variable Inequalities
- ✓ One– Step Inequalities
- ✓ Two– Step Inequalities
- ✓ Multi– Step Inequalities

Graphing Single–Variable Inequalities

Helpful Hints

– Isolate the variable.

– Find the value of the inequality on the number line.

– For less than or greater than draw open circle on the value of the variable.

– If there is an equal sign too, then use filled circle.

– Draw a line to the right direction.

✎ *Draw a graph for each inequality.*

1) $-2 > x$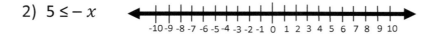

2) $5 \leq -x$

3) $x > 7$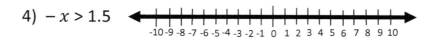

4) $-x > 1.5$

One–Step Inequalities

Helpful Hints
- Isolate the variable.
- For dividing both sides by negative numbers, flip the direction of the inequality sign.

Example:

$x + 4 \geq 11$

$x \geq 7$

✍ *Solve each inequality and graph it.*

1) $x + 9 \geq 11$

2) $x - 4 \leq 2$

3) $6x \geq 36$

4) $7 + x < 16$

5) $x + 8 \leq 1$

6) $3x > 12$

7) $3x < 24$

Two–Step Inequalities

Helpful Hints	– Isolate the variable. – For dividing both sides by negative numbers, flip the direction of the of the inequality sign. – Simplify using the inverse of addition or subtraction. – Simplify further by using the inverse of multiplication or division.	Example: $2x + 9 \geq 11$ $2x \geq 2$ $x \geq 1$

✎ *Solve each inequality and graph it.*

1) $3x - 4 \leq 5$

2) $2x - 2 \leq 6$

3) $4x - 4 \leq 8$

4) $3x + 6 \geq 12$

5) $6x - 5 \geq 19$

6) $2x - 4 \leq 6$

7) $8x - 4 \leq 4$

8) $6x + 4 \leq 10$

9) $5x + 4 \leq 9$

10) $7x - 4 \leq 3$

11) $4x - 19 < 19$

12) $2x - 3 < 21$

13) $7 + 4x \geq 19$

14) $9 + 4x < 21$

15) $3 + 2x \geq 19$

16) $6 + 4x < 22$

Multi–Step Inequalities

> **Helpful Hints**
>
> − Isolate the variable.
>
> − Simplify using the inverse of addition or subtraction.
>
> − Simplify further by using the inverse of multiplication or division.
>
> **Example:**
>
> $\dfrac{7x+1}{3} \geq 5$
>
> $7x + 1 \geq 15$
>
> $7x \geq 14$
>
> $x \geq 7$

✎ Solve each inequality.

1) $\dfrac{9x}{7} - 7 < 2$

2) $\dfrac{4x+8}{2} \leq 12$

3) $\dfrac{3x-8}{7} > 1$

4) $-3(x-7) > 21$

5) $4 + \dfrac{x}{3} < 7$

6) $\dfrac{2x+6}{4} \leq 10$

Test Preparation

1) A football team had $20,000 to spend on supplies. The team spent $14,000 on new balls. New sport shoes cost $120 each. Which of the following inequalities represent how many new shoes the team can purchase.

   A. $120x + 14{,}000 \leq 20{,}000$

   B. $120x + 14{,}000 \geq 20{,}000$

   C. $14{,}000x + 120 \leq 20{,}000$

   D. $14{,}000x + 12{,}0 \geq 20{,}000$

2) In 1999, the average worker's income increased $2,000 per year starting from $24,000 annual salary. Which equation represents income greater than average? (I = income, x = number of years after 1999)

   A. I > 2000 x + 24000

   B. I > − 2000 x + 24000

   C. I < −2000 x + 24000

   D. I < 2000 x − 24000

3) Which of the following graphs represents the compound inequality $-2 \leq 2x - 4 < 8$?

A.

B.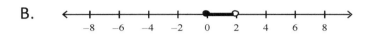

C.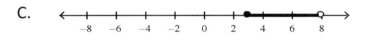

D.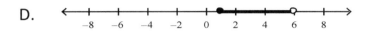

Answers of Worksheets – Chapter 8

Graphing Single–Variable Inequalities

1) $-2 > x$

2) $x \leq -5$

3) $x > 7$

4) $-1.5 > x$

One–Step Inequalities

1) $x + 9 \geq 11$

2) $x - 4 \leq 2$

3) $6x \geq 36$

4) $7 + x < 16$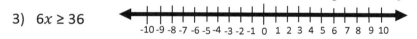

5) $x + 8 \leq 1$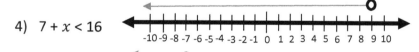

6) $3x > 12$

7) $3x < 24$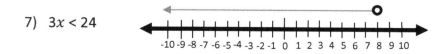

136

Two–Step inequalities

1) $x \leq 3$
2) $x \leq 4$
3) $x \leq 3$
4) $x \geq 2$
5) $x \geq 4$
6) $x \leq 5$
7) $x \leq 1$
8) $x \leq 1$
9) $x \leq 1$
10) $x \leq 1$
11) $x < 9.5$
12) $x < 12$
13) $x \geq 3$
14) $x < 3$
15) $x \geq 8$
16) $x < 4$

Multi–Step inequalities

1) $x < 7$
2) $x \leq 4$
3) $x > 5$
4) $x < 0$
5) $x < 9$
6) $x \leq 17$

Test Preparation Answers

1) Choice A is correct

Let x be the number of new shoes the team can purchase. Therefore, the team can purchase $120\,x$.

The team had $20,000 and spent $14000. Now the team can spend on new shoes $6000 at most.

Now, write the inequality:

$120x + 14.000 \leq 20.000$

2) Choice A is correct

Let x be the number of years. Therefore, $2,000 per year equals $2000x$.

starting from $24,000 annual salary means you should add that amount to $2000x$.

Income more than that is:

I > 2000x + 24000

3) Choice D is correct

$-2 \leq 2x - 4 < 8 \rightarrow$ (add 4 all sides) $-2 + 4 \leq 2x < 8 + 4 \rightarrow 2 \leq 2x < 12$
$\rightarrow$ (divide all sides by 2) $1 \leq x < 6$

Chapter 9: Exponents and Radicals

Topics that you'll learn in this chapter:

- ✓ Multiplication Property of Exponents
- ✓ Division Property of Exponents
- ✓ Powers of Products and Quotients
- ✓ Zero and Negative Exponents
- ✓ Negative Exponents and Negative Bases
- ✓ Writing Scientific Notation
- ✓ Square Roots

Multiplication Property of Exponents

Helpful Hints

Exponents rules

$x^a \cdot x^b = x^{a+b}$ $x^a/x^b = x^{a-b}$

$1/x^b = x^{-b}$ $(x^a)^b = x^{a \cdot b}$

$(xy)^a = x^a \cdot y^a$

Example:

$(x^2y)^3 = x^6y^3$

✏️ *Simplify.*

1) $4^2 \cdot 4^2$

2) $2 \cdot 2^2 \cdot 2^2$

3) $3^2 \cdot 3^2$

4) $3x^3 \cdot x$

5) $12x^4 \cdot 3x$

6) $6x \cdot 2x^2$

7) $5x^4 \cdot 5x^4$

8) $6x^2 \cdot 6x^3y^4$

9) $7x^2y^5 \cdot 9xy^3$

10) $7xy^4 \cdot 4x^3y^3$

11) $(2x^2)^2$

12) $3x^5y^3 \cdot 8x^2y^3$

13) $7x^3 \cdot 10y^3x^5 \cdot 8yx^3$

14) $(x^4)^3$

15) $(2x^2)^4$

16) $(x^2)^3$

17) $(6x)^2$

18) $3x^4y^5 \cdot 7x^2y^3$

Division Property of Exponents

Helpful Hints

$\dfrac{x^a}{x^b} = x^{a-b}, x \neq 0$

Example:

$\dfrac{x^{12}}{x^5} = x^7$

✏️ **Simplify.**

1) $\dfrac{5^5}{5}$

2) $\dfrac{3}{3^5}$

3) $\dfrac{2^2}{2^3}$

4) $\dfrac{2^4}{2^2}$

5) $\dfrac{x}{x^3}$

6) $\dfrac{3x^3}{9x^4}$

7) $\dfrac{2x^{-5}}{9x^{-2}}$

8) $\dfrac{21x^8}{7x^3}$

9) $\dfrac{7x^6}{4x^7}$

10) $\dfrac{6x^2}{4x^3}$

11) $\dfrac{5x}{10x^3}$

12) $\dfrac{3x^3}{2x^5}$

13) $\dfrac{12x^3}{14x^6}$

14) $\dfrac{12x^3}{9y^8}$

15) $\dfrac{25xy^4}{5x^6y^2}$

16) $\dfrac{2x^4}{7x}$

17) $\dfrac{16x^2y^8}{4x^3}$

18) $\dfrac{12x^4}{15x^7y^9}$

19) $\dfrac{12yx^4}{10yx^8}$

20) $\dfrac{16x^4y}{9x^8y^2}$

21) $\dfrac{5x^8}{20x^8}$

Powers of Products and Quotients

Helpful Hints

For any nonzero numbers a and b and any integer x, $(ab)^x = a^x \cdot b^x$.

Example:

$(2x^2 \cdot y^3)^2 =$

$4x^2 \cdot y^6$

✎ *Simplify.*

1) $(2x^3)^4$

2) $(4xy^4)^2$

3) $(5x^4)^2$

4) $(11x^5)^2$

5) $(4x^2y^4)^4$

6) $(2x^4y^4)^3$

7) $(3x^2y^2)^2$

8) $(3x^4y^3)^4$

9) $(2x^6y^8)^2$

10) $(12x\ 3x)^3$

11) $(2x^9\ x^6)^3$

12) $(5x^{10}y^3)^3$

13) $(4x^3\ x^2)^2$

14) $(3x^3\ 5x)^2$

15) $(10x^{11}y^3)^2$

16) $(9x^7\ y^5)^2$

17) $(4x^4y^6)^5$

18) $(4x^4)^2$

19) $(3x\ 4y^3)^2$

20) $(9x^2y)^3$

21) $(12x^2y^5)^2$

Zero and Negative Exponents

Helpful Hints

A negative exponent simply means that the base is on the wrong side of the fraction line, so you need to flip the base to the other side. For instance, "x^{-2}" (pronounced as "ecks to the minus two") just means "x^2" but underneath, as in $\frac{1}{x^2}$

Example:

$5^{-2} = \frac{1}{25}$

✎ *Evaluate the following expressions.*

1) 8^{-2}

2) 2^{-4}

3) 10^{-2}

4) 5^{-3}

5) 22^{-1}

6) 9^{-1}

7) 3^{-2}

8) 4^{-2}

9) 5^{-2}

10) 35^{-1}

11) 6^{-3}

12) 0^{15}

13) 10^{-9}

14) 3^{-4}

15) 5^{-2}

16) 2^{-3}

17) 3^{-3}

18) 8^{-1}

19) 7^{-3}

20) 6^{-2}

21) $(\frac{2}{3})^{-2}$

22) $(\frac{1}{5})^{-3}$

23) $(\frac{1}{2})^{-8}$

24) $(\frac{2}{5})^{-3}$

Negative Exponents and Negative Bases

Helpful Hints

– Make the power positive. A negative exponent is the reciprocal of that number with a positive exponent.

– The parenthesis is important!

– -5^{-2} is not the same as $(-5)^{-2}$

$-5^{-2} = -\frac{1}{5^2}$ and $(-5)^{-2} = +\frac{1}{5^2}$

Example:

$2x^{-3} = \frac{2}{x^3}$

✎ *Simplify.*

1) -6^{-1}

2) $-4x^{-3}$

3) $-\frac{5x}{x^{-3}}$

4) $-\frac{a^{-3}}{b^{-2}}$

5) $-\frac{5}{x^{-3}}$

6) $\frac{7b}{-9c^{-4}}$

7) $-\frac{5n^{-2}}{10p^{-3}}$

8) $\frac{4ab^{-2}}{-3c^{-2}}$

9) $-12x^2y^{-3}$

10) $\left(-\frac{1}{3}\right)^{-2}$

11) $\left(-\frac{3}{4}\right)^{-2}$

12) $\left(\frac{3a}{2c}\right)^{-2}$

13) $\left(-\frac{5x}{3yz}\right)^{-3}$

14) $-\frac{2x}{a^{-4}}$

Writing Scientific Notation

Helpful Hints

− It is used to write very big or very small numbers in decimal form.

− In scientific notation all numbers are written in the form of:

$$m \times 10^n$$

Decimal notation	Scientific notation
5	5×10^0
−25,000	$−2.5 \times 10^4$
0.5	5×10^{-1}
2,122.456	$2,122456 \times 10^3$

✎ *Write each number in scientific notation.*

1) 91×10^3

2) 60

3) 2000000

4) 0.0000006

5) 354000

6) 0.000325

7) 2.5

8) 0.00023

9) 56000000

10) 2000000

11) 78000000

12) 0.0000022

13) 0.00012

14) 0.004

15) 78

16) 1600

17) 1450

18) 130000

19) 60

20) 0.113

21) 0.02

Square Roots

Helpful Hints

— A square root of x is a number r whose square is: $r^2 = x$

r is a square root of x.

Example:

$\sqrt{4} = 2$

✎ Find the value each square root.

1) $\sqrt{1}$

2) $\sqrt{4}$

3) $\sqrt{9}$

4) $\sqrt{25}$

5) $\sqrt{16}$

6) $\sqrt{49}$

7) $\sqrt{36}$

8) $\sqrt{0}$

9) $\sqrt{64}$

10) $\sqrt{81}$

11) $\sqrt{121}$

12) $\sqrt{225}$

13) $\sqrt{144}$

14) $\sqrt{100}$

15) $\sqrt{256}$

16) $\sqrt{289}$

17) $\sqrt{324}$

18) $\sqrt{400}$

19) $\sqrt{900}$

20) $\sqrt{529}$

21) $\sqrt{90}$

Test Preparation

1) What is the value of 5^4?

   Write your answer in the box below.

   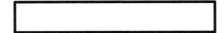

2) How is this number written in scientific notation?

   0.00002389

   A. 2.389×10^{-5}

   B. 23.89×10^{6}

   C. 0.2389×10^{-4}

   D. 2389×10^{-8}

3) What is the value of 3^6?

   Write your answer in the box below.

   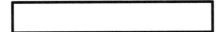

4) How is this number written in scientific notation?

$$0.0050468$$

A. 5.0468×10^{-3}

B. 5.0468×10^{3}

C. 0.50468×10^{-2}

D. 50468×10^{-7}

Answers of Worksheets – Chapter 9

Multiplication Property of Exponents

1) 4^4
2) 2^5
3) 3^4
4) $3x^4$
5) $36x^5$
6) $12x^3$
7) $25x^8$
8) $36x^5y^4$
9) $63x^3y^8$
10) $28x^4y^7$
11) $4x^4$
12) $24x^7y^6$
13) $560x^{11}y^4$
14) x^{12}
15) $16x^8$
16) x^6
17) $36x^2$
18) $21x^6y^8$

Division Property of Exponents

1) 5^4
2) $\frac{1}{3^4}$
3) $\frac{1}{2}$
4) 2^2
5) $\frac{1}{x^2}$
6) $\frac{1}{3x}$
7) $\frac{2}{9x^3}$
8) $3x^5$
9) $\frac{7}{4x}$
10) $\frac{3}{2x}$
11) $\frac{1}{2x^2}$
12) $\frac{3}{2x^2}$
13) $\frac{6}{7x^3}$
14) $\frac{4x^3}{3y^8}$
15) $\frac{5y^2}{x^5}$
16) $\frac{2x^3}{7}$
17) $\frac{4y^8}{x}$
18) $\frac{4}{5x^3y^9}$
19) $\frac{6}{5x^4}$
20) $\frac{16}{9x^4y}$
21) $\frac{1}{4}$

Powers of Products and Quotients

1) $16x^{12}$
2) $16x^2y^8$
3) $25x^8$
4) $121x^{10}$
5) $256x^8y^{16}$
6) $8x^{12}y^{12}$
7) $9x^4y^4$
8) $81x^{16}y^{12}$
9) $4x^{12}y^{16}$
10) $46,656x^6$
11) $8x^{45}$
12) $125x^{30}y^9$
13) $16x^{10}$
14) $225x^8$
15) $100x^{22}y^6$
16) $81x^{14}y^{10}$
17) $1,024x^{20}y^{30}$
18) $16x^8$

19) $144x^2y^6$ 20) $729x^6y^3$ 21) $144x^4y^{10}$

Zero and Negative Exponents

1) $\frac{1}{64}$

2) $\frac{1}{16}$

3) $\frac{1}{100}$

4) $\frac{1}{125}$

5) $\frac{1}{22}$

6) $\frac{1}{9}$

7) $\frac{1}{9}$

8) $\frac{1}{16}$

9) $\frac{1}{25}$

10) $\frac{1}{35}$

11) $\frac{1}{216}$

12) 0

13) $\frac{1}{1000000000}$

14) $\frac{1}{81}$

15) $\frac{1}{25}$

16) $\frac{1}{8}$

17) $\frac{1}{27}$

18) $\frac{1}{8}$

19) $\frac{1}{343}$

20) $\frac{1}{36}$

21) $\frac{9}{4}$

22) 125

23) 256

24) $\frac{125}{8}$

Negative Exponents and Negative Bases

1) $-\frac{1}{6}$

2) $-\frac{4}{x^3}$

3) $-5x^4$

4) $-\frac{b^2}{a^3}$

5) $-5x^3$

6) $-\frac{7bc^4}{9}$

7) $-\frac{p^3}{2n^2}$

8) $-\frac{4ac^2}{3b^2}$

9) $-\frac{12x^2}{y^3}$

10) 9

11) $\frac{16}{9}$

12) $\frac{4c^2}{9a^2}$

13) $-\frac{27y^3z^3}{125x^3}$

14) $-2xa^4$

Writing Scientific Notation

1) 9.1×10^4

2) 6×10^1

3) 2×10^6

4) 6×10^{-7}

5) 3.54×10^5

6) 3.25×10^{-4}

7) 2.5×10^0

8) 2.3×10^{-4}

9) 5.6×10^7

10) 2×10^6

11) 7.8×10^7

12) 2.2×10^{-6}

13) 1.2×10^{-4}
14) 4×10^{-3}
15) 7.8×10^{1}
16) 1.6×10^{3}
17) 1.45×10^{3}
18) 1.3×10^{5}
19) 6×10^{1}
20) 1.13×10^{-1}
21) 2×10^{-2}

Square Roots

1) 1
2) 2
3) 3
4) 5
5) 4
6) 7
7) 6
8) 0
9) 8
10) 9
11) 11
12) 15
13) 12
14) 10
15) 16
16) 17
17) 18
18) 20
19) 30
20) 23
21) $3\sqrt{10}$

Test Preparation Answers

1) The answer is 625.

$5^4 = 5 \times 5 \times 5 \times 5 = 625$

2) Choice A is correct.

$0.00002389 = \dfrac{2.389}{100000} \Rightarrow 2.389 \times 10^{-5}$

3) The answer is 729.

$3^6 = 3 \times 3 \times 3 \times 3 \times 3 \times 3 = 729$

4) Choice A is correct

$0.0050468 = \dfrac{5.0468}{1000} \Rightarrow 5.0468 \times 10^{-3}$

Chapter 10: Measurements

Topics that you'll learn in this chapter:

- ✓ Inches & Centimeters
- ✓ Metric units
- ✓ Distance Measurement
- ✓ Weight Measurement

Inches and Centimeters

Helpful Hints

1 inch = 2.5 cm

1 foot = 12 inches

1 yard = 3 feet

1 yard = 36 inches

1 inch = 0.0254 m

Example:

18 inches = 0.4572 m

✎ **Convert to the units.**

1 inch = 2.5 cm

1) 25 cm = _____ inches

2) 11 inches = _____ cm

3) 1 m = _____ inches

4) 80 inches = _____ m

5) 200 cm = _____ m

6) 5 m = _____ cm

7) 4 feet = _____ inches

8) 10 yards = _____ inches

9) 16 feet = _____ inches

10) 48 inches = _____ Feet

11) 4 inches = _____ cm

12) 12.5 cm = _____ inches

13) 6 feet: _____ inches

14) 10 feet: _____ inches

15) 12 yards: _____ feet

16) 7 yards: _____ feet

Metric Units

Helpful Hints

1 m = 100 cm
1 cm = 10 mm
1 m = 1000 mm
1 km = 1000 m

Example:

12 cm = 0.12 m

✎ **Convert to the units.**

1) 4 mm = _____ cm

2) 0.6 m = _____ mm

3) 2 m = _____ cm

4) 0.03 km = _____ m

5) 3000 mm = _____ km

6) 5 cm = _____ m

7) 0.03 m = _____ cm

8) 1000 mm = _____ km

9) 600 mm = _____ m

10) 0.77 km = _____ mm

11) 0.08 km = _____ m

12) 0.30 m = _____ cm

13) 400 m = _____ km

14) 5000 cm = _____ km

15) 40 mm = _____ cm

16) 800 m = _____ km

Distance Measurement

Helpful Hints

1 mile = 5280 ft
1 mile = 1760 yd
1 mile = 1609.34 m

Example:

10 miles = 52800 ft

✎ Convert to the new units.

1) 2 mi = _____ ft

2) 21 mi = _____ ft

3) 6 mi = _____ ft

4) 3 mi = _____ yd

5) 72 mi = _____ ft

6) 41 mi = _____ yd

7) 62 mi = _____ yd

8) 39 mi = _____ yd

9) 7 mi = _____ yd

10) 94 mi = _____ yd

11) 87 mi = _____ yd

12) 23 mi = _____ yd

13) 2 mi = _____ m

14) 5 mi = _____ m

15) 6 mi = _____ m

16) 3 mi = _____ m

Weight Measurement

Helpful Hints

1 kg = 1000g

Example:

2000 g = 2 kg

✎ **Convert to grams.**

1) 0.5 kg = _____ g

2) 3.2 kg = _____ g

3) 8.2 kg = _____ g

4) 9.2 kg = _____ g

5) 35 kg = _____ g

6) 87 kg = _____ g

7) 45 kg = _____ g

8) 15 kg = _____ g

9) 0.32 kg = _____ g

10) 81 kg = _____ g

✎ **Convert to kilograms.**

11) 200,000 g = _____ kg

12) 30,000 g = _____ kg

13) 800,000 g = _____ kg

14) 20,000 g = _____ kg

15) 40,000 g = _____ kg

16) 500,000 g = _____ kg

Test Preparation

1) 12 yards 4 feet and 2 inches equals to how many inches?

    A. 96
    B. 432
    C. 482
    D. 578

2) A rope weighs 800 grams per meter of length. What is the weight in kilograms of 12.2 meters of this rope? (1 kilograms = 1000 grams)

   A. 0.0976

   B. 0.976

   C. 9.76

   D. 9,760

3) A house floor has a perimeter of 4,221 feet. What is the perimeter of the floor in yards?

   Write your answer in the box below.

   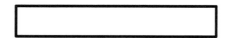

Answers of Worksheets – Chapter 10

Inches & Centimeters

1) 25 cm = 9.84 inches
2) 11 inch = 27.94 cm
3) 1 m = 39.37 inches
4) 80 inch = 2.03 m
5) 200 cm = 2 m
6) 5 m = 500 cm
7) 4 feet = 48 inches
8) 10 yards = 360 inches
9) 16 feet = 192 inches
10) 48 inches = 4 Feet
11) 4 inch = 10.16 cm
12) 12.5 cm = 4.92 inches
13) 6 feet: 72 inches
14) 10 feet: 120 inches
15) 12 yards: 36 feet
16) 7 yards: 21 feet

Metric Units

1) 4 mm = 0.4 cm
2) 0.6 m = 600 mm
3) 2 m = 200 cm
4) 0.03 km = 30 m
5) 3000 mm = 0.003 km
6) 5 cm = 0.05 m
7) 0.03 m = 3 cm
8) 1000 mm = 0.001 km
9) 600 mm = 0.6 m
10) 0.77 km = 770,000 mm
11) 0.08 km = 80 m
12) 0.30 m = 30 cm
13) 400 m = 0.4 km
14) 5000 cm = 0.05 km
15) 40 mm = 4 cm
16) 800 m = 0.8 km

Distance Measurement

1) 21 mi = 110880 ft
2) 6 mi = 31680 ft
3) 3 mi = 5280 yd
4) 72 mi = 380160 ft
5) 41 mi = 72160 yd
6) 62 mi = 109120 yd
7) 39 mi = 68640 yd
8) 7 mi = 12320 yd
9) 94 mi = 165440 yd
10) 87 mi = 153120 yd

11) 23 mi = 40480 yd
12) 2 mi = 3218.69 m
13) 5 mi = 8046.72 m

14) 6 mi = 9656.06 m
15) 3 mi = 4828.03 m

Weight Measurement

1) 0.5 kg = 500 g
2) 3.2 kg = 3200 g
3) 8.2 kg = 8200 g
4) 9.2 kg = 9200 g
5) 35 kg = 35000 g
6) 87 kg = 87000 g
7) 45 kg = 45000 g
8) 15 kg = 15000 g
9) 0.32 kg = 320 g
10) 81 kg = 81000 g

11) 200,000 g = 200 kg
12) 30,000 g = 30 kg
13) 800,000 g = 800 kg
14) 20,000 g = 20 kg
15) 40,000 g = 40 kg
16) 500,000 g = 500 kg

Test Preparation Answers

1) Choice C is correct

12 Yards = (12×36) 432 inches

4 feet = (4×12) 48 inches

12 yards + 4 feet + 2 inches = 432 + 48 + 2 = 482

2) Choice C is correct

The weighs of rope per meter of length = 800 grams. We use ratio to find answer (Let x be the amount of weight):

$$\frac{800 \text{ grams}}{1 \text{ meter}} = \frac{x \text{ grams}}{12.2 \text{ meter}} \Rightarrow x = 9760 \text{ grams } x = 9.760 \text{ kilograms}$$

3) The answer is 1407.

1 yard = 3 feet

$4221 \div 3 = 1407$

Chapter 11: Plane Figures

Topics that you'll learn in this chapter:

- ✓ The Pythagorean Theorem
- ✓ Area of Triangles
- ✓ Perimeter of Polygons
- ✓ Area and Circumference of Circles
- ✓ Area of Squares, Rectangles, and Parallelograms
- ✓ Area of Trapezoids

The Pythagorean Theorem

Helpful Hints

— In any right triangle:

$a^2 + b^2 = c^2$

Example:

Missing side = 5

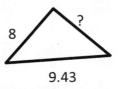

9.43

✎ **Do the following lengths form a right triangle?**

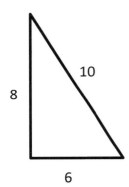

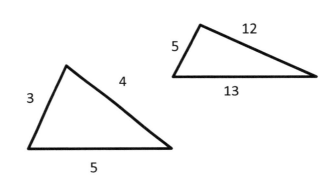

✎ **Find each missing length to the nearest tenth.**

4)

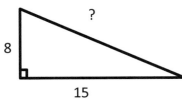

5)   6)

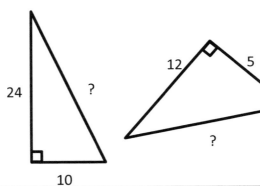

PSSA Mathematics Workbook For Grade 6

Area of Triangles

Helpful Hints   Area = $\frac{1}{2}$ (base × height)

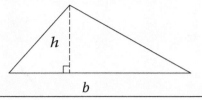

✏️ Find the area of each.

1)
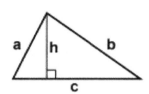

c = 9 mi

h = 3.7 mi

2)
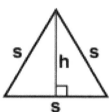

s = 14 m

h = 12.2 m

3)
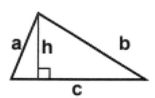

a = 5 m

b = 11 m

c = 14 m

h = 4 m

4)
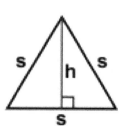

s = 10 m

h = 8.6 m

164   www.EffortlessMath.com

Perimeter of Polygons

Helpful Hints

Perimeter of a square = 4s

Perimeter of a rectangle = $2(l + w)$

Perimeter of trapezoid = a + b + c + d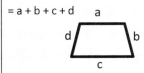

Perimeter of Pentagon = 6a

Perimeter of a parallelogram = $2(l + w)$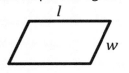

Example:

P = 18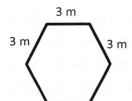

✏️ *Find the perimeter of each shape.*

1)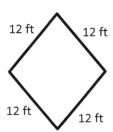

2)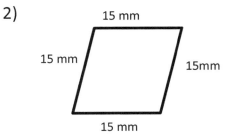

3)

4)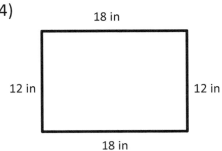

Area and Circumference of Circles

Helpful Hints

Area = πr²

Circumference = 2πr

Example:

If the radius of a circle is 3, then:

Area = 28.27

Circumference = 18.85

✏️ **Find the area and circumference of each.** (π = 3.14)

1)

2)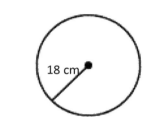

3)

4)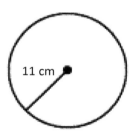

5)

6)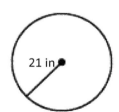

Area of Squares, Rectangles, and Parallelograms

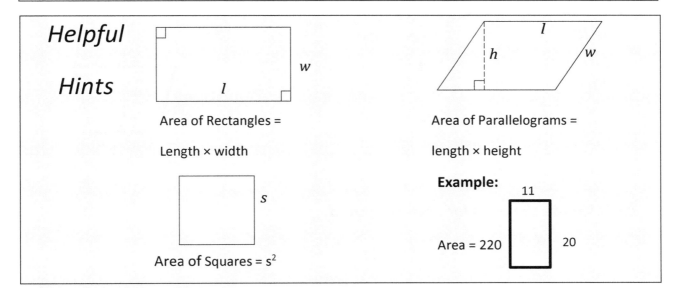

Helpful Hints

Area of Rectangles = Length × width

Area of Squares = s^2

Area of Parallelograms = length × height

Example:
Area = 220

✎ **Find the area of each.**

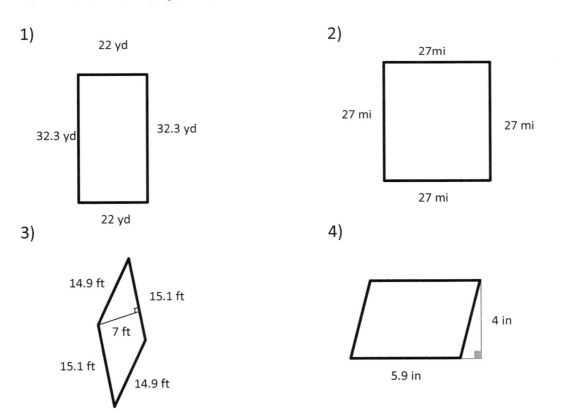

1) 22 yd, 32.3 yd

2) 27 mi square

3) 14.9 ft, 15.1 ft, 7 ft

4) 5.9 in, 4 in

Area of Trapezoids

Helpful Hints $A = \frac{1}{2}h(b_1 + b_2)$

Example:

$A = 252$ cm^2

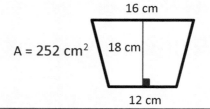

✏️ **Calculate the area for each trapezoid.**

1)

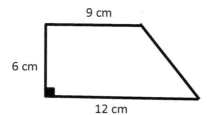

2)

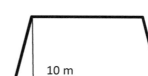

3)

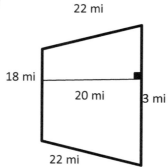

4)

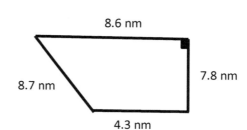

168

Test Preparation

1) In a triangle ABC the measure of angle ACB is 68° and the measure of angle CAB is 52°. What is the measure of angle ABC?

   Write your answer in the box below.

2) The perimeter of a rectangular yard is 60 meters. What is its length if its width is 10 meters?

   A. 10 meters

   B. 18 meters

   C. 20 meters

   D. 24 meters

3) The radius of the following cylinder is 4 inches and its height is 10 inches. What is the volume of the cylinder?

   Write your answer in the box below. (π equals 3.14) (Round your answer to the nearest whole number)

4) The perimeter of the trapezoid below is 52. What is its area?

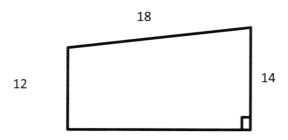

Write your answer in the box below.

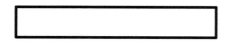

5) The area of a circle is 64 π. What is the circumference of the circle?

A. 8 π

B. 16 π

C. 32 π

D. 64 π

6) The length of a rectangle is 12 inches long and its area is 96 square inches. What is the perimeter of the rectangle?

Write your answer in the box below.

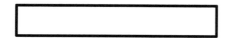

7) The perimeter of the trapezoid below is 36 cm. What is its area?

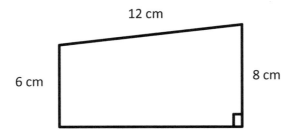

A. 26

B. 42

C. 48

D. 70

8) What is the perimeter of a square that has an area of 169 square inches?

Write your answer in the box below.

Answers of Worksheets – Chapter 11

The Pythagorean Theorem

1) yes
2) yes
3) yes
4) 17
5) 26
6) 13

Area of Triangles

1) 16.65 mi^2
2) 56 m^2
3) 85.4 m^2
4) 43 m^2

Perimeter of Polygons

1) 30 m
2) 60 mm
3) 48 ft
4) 60 in

Area and Circumference of Circles

1) Area: 50.24 in^2, Circumference: 25.12 in
2) Area: 1,017.36 cm^2, Circumference: 113.04 cm
3) Area: 78.5 m^2, Circumference: 31.4 m
4) Area: 379.94 cm^2, Circumference: 69.08 cm
5) Area: 200.96 km^2, Circumference: 50.2 km
6) Area: 1,384.74 km^2, Circumference: 131.88 km

Area of Squares, Rectangles, and Parallelograms

1) 710.6 yd^2
2) 729 mi^2
3) 105.7 ft^2
4) 23.6 in^2

Area of Trapezoids

1) 63 cm^2
2) 192 m^2
3) 451 mi^2
4) 50.31 nm^2

Test Preparation Answers

1) **The answer is 60.**

The whole angles in every triangle are: 180° and Let x be the number of new angle so:

180 = 68 + 52 + x ⇒ $x = 60°$

2) **Choice C is correct**

Let x be the length, and its $width = 10$

Perimeter of the rectangle is 2(width + length) = $2(10 + x) = 60 \Rightarrow 10 + x = 30 \Rightarrow x = 20$

Length of the rectangle is 10 meters.

3) **The answer is 502.**

The volume of the cylinder: $\pi r^2 h$

The volume of the cylinder: (3.14) × (4)² × 10 = 502.4 ≅ 502

4) **The answer is 104.**

The perimeter of the trapezoid = the sum of the lengths of its four sides

So: 52 = 12+ 18+ 14+ $x \Rightarrow x$ =8

The area of the trapezoid = the sum of its bases, multiply the half of its height

So The area of the trapezoid = (12+14) × $\frac{8}{2}$ = 104

5) Choice B is correct

Use the formula of areas of circles.

Area = $\pi r^2 \Rightarrow 64\pi = \pi r^2 \Rightarrow 64 = r^2 \Rightarrow r = 8$

Radius of the circle is 8. Now, use the circumference formula:

Circumference = $2\pi r = 2\pi(8) = 16\pi$

6) The answer is 40.

Use the formula of areas of rectangles.

Area: length plus width $\Rightarrow 96 = 12 \times$ width $\Rightarrow$ width = 8

Use the formula of perimeter of rectangles.

Perimeter: 2(length + width) $\Rightarrow 2(12 + 8) = 40$

7) Choice D is correct

The perimeter of the trapezoid is 36 cm.

Therefore, the missing side (height) is = $36 - 8 - 12 - 6 = 10$

Area of a trapezoid: A = $\frac{1}{2} h (b_1 + b_2) = \frac{1}{2}(10)(6+8) = 70$

8) The answer is 52.

Use the area of a square formula.

$S = a^2 \Rightarrow 169 = a^2 \Rightarrow a = 13$

Use the perimeter of a square formula.

$P = 4a \Rightarrow p = 4 \times 13 \Rightarrow p = 52$

Chapter 12: Solid Figures

Topics that you'll learn in this chapter:

- ✓ Volume of Cubes
- ✓ Volume of Rectangle Prisms
- ✓ Surface Area of Cubes
- ✓ Surface Area of Rectangle Prisms

PSSA Mathematics Workbook For Grade 6

Volume of Cubes

Helpful Hints

− Volume is the measure of the amount of space inside of a solid figure, like a cube, ball, cylinder or pyramid.

− Volume of a cube = (one side)^3

− Volume of a rectangle prism: Length × Width × Height

✏️ *Find the volume of each.*

1)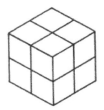

2)

3)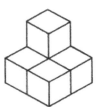

4)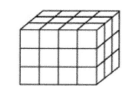

5)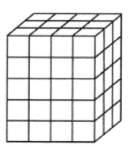

6)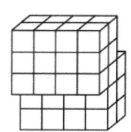

www.EffortlessMath.com

Volume of Rectangle Prisms

Helpful Hints

Volume of rectangle prism

length × width × height

Example:

10 × 5 × 8 = 400m³

✎ Find the volume of each of the rectangular prisms.

1)

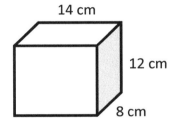

2)

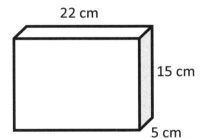

3)

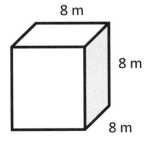

4)

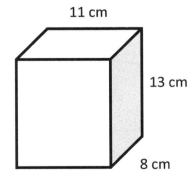

Surface Area of Cubes

Helpful Hints

Surface Area of a cube =

$6 \times$ (one side of the cube)^2

Example:

$6 \times 4^2 = 96 m^2$

✎ Find the surface of each cube.

1)

6 mm

2)

9 mm

3)

10 cm

4)

8 m

5)

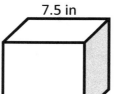

7.5 in

6)

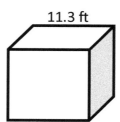

11.3 ft

178

Surface Area of a Rectangle Prism

Helpful Hints

Surface Area of a Rectangle Prism Formula:

SA =2 [(width × length) + (height × length) + width × height)]

✎ **Find the surface of each prism.**

1)

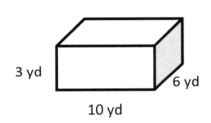

2)

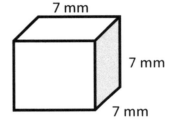

3)

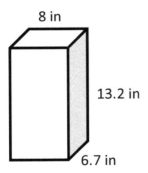

4)

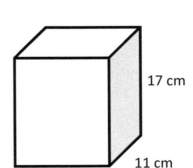

179

PSSA Mathematics Workbook For Grade 6

Volume of a Cylinder

Helpful Hints

Volume of Cylinder Formula = π(radius)² × height

π = 3.14

✏️ **Find the volume of each cylinder.** (π = 3.14)

1)

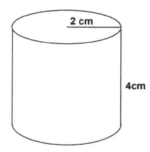

2)

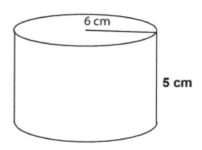

3)

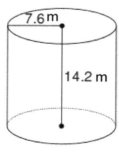

4)

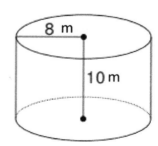

180   www.EffortlessMath.com

Surface Area of a Cylinder

Helpful Hints

Surface area of a cylinder

$SA = 2\pi r^2 + 2\pi rh$

Example:

Surface area

= 1727

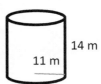

✏️ **Find the surface of each cylinder.** ($\pi = 3.14$)

1)

2)

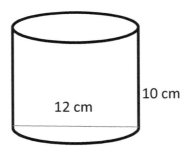

3)

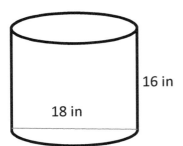

4)

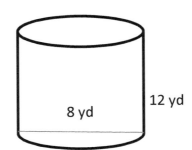

Test Preparation

1) In a party, 6 soft drinks are required for every 9 guests. If there are 171 guests, how many soft drink is required?

   A. 9
   B. 27
   C. 114
   D. 171

2) A swimming pool holds 2,000 cubic feet of water. The swimming pool is 25 feet long and 10 feet wide. How deep is the swimming pool?

   Write your answer in the box below. (Don't write the measurement)

   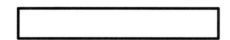

3) What is the volume of a cube whose side is 4 cm?

   A. 16 cm³
   B. 32 cm³
   C. 36 cm³
   D. 64 cm³

4) What is the volume of the cylinder below?

A. 48 π in²

B. 57 π in²

C. 66 π in²

D. 72 π in²

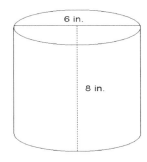

5) What is the volume of a box with the following dimensions?

Hight = 4 cm   Width = 5 cm   Length = 6 cm

A. 15 cm³
B. 60 cm³
C. 90 cm³
D. 120 cm³

Answers of Worksheets – Chapter 12

Volumes of Cubes

1) 8
2) 4
3) 5
4) 36
5) 60
6) 44

Volume of Rectangle Prisms

1) 1344 cm^3
2) 1650 cm^3
3) 512 m^3
4) 1144 cm^3

Surface Area of a Cube

1) 216 mm^2
2) 486 mm^2
3) 600 cm^2
4) 384 m^2
5) 337.5 in^2
6) 766.14 ft^2

Surface Area of a Prism

1) 216 yd^2
2) 294 mm^2
3) 495.28 in^2
4) 1326 cm^2

Volume of a Cylinder

1) 50.24 cm^3
2) 565.2 cm^3
3) 2,575.403 m^3
4) 2009.6 m^3

Surface Area of a Cylinder

1) 301.44 ft^2
2) 602.88 cm^2
3) 1413 in^2
4) 401.92 yd^2

Test Preparation Answers

1) **Choice D is correct**

volume of rectangle prism = length × width × height

x = 10m × 4m × 5m ⇒ x = 200 m³

2) **The answer is 8.**

Use formula of rectangle prism volume.

V = (length) (width) (height) ⇒ 2000 = (25) (10) (height) ⇒

height = 2000 ÷ 250 = 8

3) **Choice D is correct.**

Use volume of a cube formula.

V= a³ ⇒ V= 4³ ⇒ V= 64

4) **Choice D is correct.**

Use volume of a cylinder formula.

V= π r²h ⇒ V= π (3)²in× 8in ⇒ V=72 π in²

5) **Choice D is correct**

Volume of a box = length × width × height = 4 × 5 × 6 = 120

Chapter 13: Statistics

Topics that you'll learn in this chapter:

- ✓ Mean, Median, Mode, and Range of the Given Data
- ✓ First Quartile, Second Quartile and Third Quartile of the Given Data
- ✓ Bar Graph
- ✓ Box and Whisker Plots
- ✓ Stem–And–Leaf Plot
- ✓ The Pie Graph or Circle Graph
- ✓ Scatter Plots

Mean, Median, Mode, and Range of the Given Data

Helpful Hints

- Mean: $\dfrac{\text{sum of the data}}{\text{of data entires}}$
- Mode: value in the list that appears most often
- Range: largest value − smallest value

Example:

22, 16, 12, 9, 7, 6, 4, 6

Mean = 10.25

Mod = 6

Range = 18

✍ *Find Mean, Median, Mode, and Range of the Given Data.*

1) 7, 2, 5, 1, 1, 2

2) 2, 2, 2, 3, 6, 3, 7, 4

3) 9, 4, 3, 1, 7, 9, 4, 6, 4

4) 8, 4, 2, 4, 3, 2, 4, 5

5) 8, 5, 7, 5, 7, 9, 8

6) 5, 1, 4, 4, 9, 2, 9, 2, 5, 1

7) 4, 1, 5, 9, 7, 7, 5, 4, 3, 5

8) 7, 5, 4, 9, 6, 7, 7, 5, 2

9) 2, 5, 5, 6, 2, 4, 7, 6, 4, 9

10) 10, 5, 2, 5, 4, 5, 8, 10

11) 5, 1, 5, 2, 2

12) 2, 3, 5, 9, 6

First Quartile, Second Quartile and Third Quartile of the Given Data

> *Helpful Hints*
>
> **Quartile 1:** It's the number halfway from smallest number and the median of the data set.
>
> **Quartile 2:** It's the median and cuts data set in half.
>
> **Quartile 3:** It's the number halfway from the median and the biggest number of the data set.

Find First Quartile, Second Quartile and Third Quartile of the Given Data.

1) 65, 8, 35, 54, 29, 42, 14, 73, 11

2) 14, 64, 30, 20, 72, 57

3) 99, 37, 83, 62, 74, 49, 59, 40

4) 33, 14, 47, 29, 52, 63, 20, 39, 74, 48

5) 23, 10, 13, 30, 26, 8, 25, 18

6) 35, 60, 20, 80, 95, 15, 40, 85, 75

Box and Whisker Plots

> *Helpful Hints*
>
> Box–and–whisker plots display data including quartiles.
> - IQR – interquartile range shows the difference from Q1 to Q3.
> - Extreme Values are the smallest and largest values in a data set.

Make box and whisker plots for the given data.

1) 73, 84, 86, 95, 68, 67, 100, 94, 77, 80, 62, 79

2) 11, 17, 22, 18, 23, 2, 3, 16, 21, 7, 8, 15, 5

3) 20, 12, 1, 24, 14, 23, 8, 2, 22, 12, 3

Bar Graph

Helpful Hints — A bar graph is a chart that presents data with bars in different heights to match with the values of the data. The bars can be graphed horizontally or vertically.

✎ **Graph the given information as a bar graph.**

Day	Hot dogs sold
Monday	90
Tuesday	70
Wednesday	30
Thursday	20
Friday	60

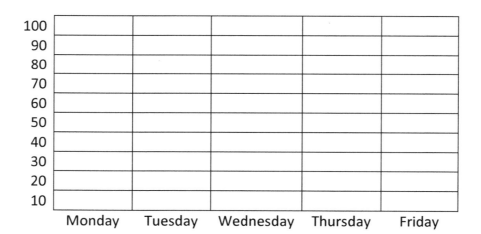

Stem–And–Leaf Plot

> **Helpful Hints**
>
> — Stem–and–leaf plots display the frequency of the values in a data set.
>
> — We can make a frequency distribution table for the values, or we can use a stem–and–leaf plot.

Example:

56, 58, 42, 48, 66, 64, 53, 69, 45, 72

Stem	leaf
4	2 5 8
5	3 6 8
6	4 6 9
7	2

✍ *Make stem ad leaf plots for the given data.*

1) 74, 88, 97, 72, 79, 86, 95, 79, 83, 91

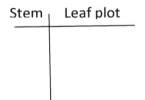

2) 37, 48, 26, 33, 49, 26, 19, 26, 48

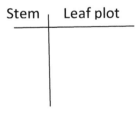

3) 58, 41, 42, 67, 54, 65, 65, 54, 69, 53

The Pie Graph or Circle Graph

Helpful Hints A Pie Chart is a circle chart divided into sectors, each sector represents the relative size of each value.

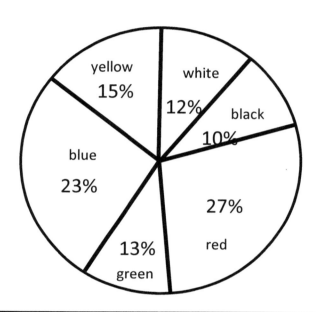

Favorite colors

1) Which color is the most?

2) What percentage of pie graph is yellow?

3) Which color is the least?

4) What percentage of pie graph is blue?

5) What percentage of pie graph is green?

Scatter Plots

Helpful Hints

A Scatter (xy) Plot shows the values with points that represent the relationship between two sets of data.

— The horizontal values are usually x and vertical data is y.

✎ Construct a scatter plot.

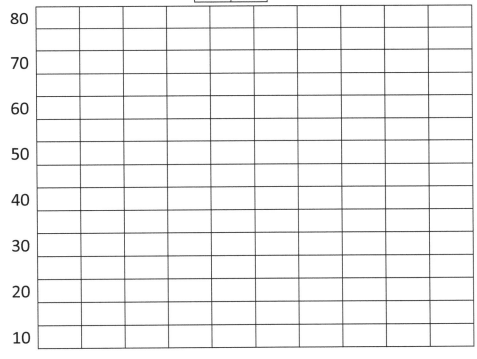

X	Y
1	20
2	40
3	50
4	60

Probability of Simple Events

> *Helpful Hints*
>
> - Probability is the likelihood of something happening in the future. It is expressed as a number between zero (can never happen) to 1 (will always happen).
> - Probability can be expressed as a fraction, a decimal, or a percent.
>
> **Example:**
>
> Probability of a flipped coins turns up 'heads'
>
> Is $0.5 = \frac{1}{2}$

✍ *Solve.*

1) A number is chosen at random from 1 to 10. Find the probability of selecting a 4 or smaller.

2) A number is chosen at random from 1 to 50. Find the probability of selecting multiples of 10.

3) A number is chosen at random from 1 to 10. Find the probability of selecting of 4 and factors of 6.

4) A number is chosen at random from 1 to 10. Find the probability of selecting a multiple of 3.

5) A number is chosen at random from 1 to 50. Find the probability of selecting prime numbers.

6) A number is chosen at random from 1 to 25. Find the probability of not selecting a composite number.

Test Preparation

1) Anita's trick–or–treat bag contains 12 pieces of chocolate, 18 suckers, 18 pieces of gum, 24 pieces of licorice. If she randomly pulls a piece of candy from her bag, what is the probability of her pulling out a piece of sucker?

   A. $\frac{1}{3}$

   B. $\frac{1}{4}$

   C. $\frac{1}{6}$

   D. $\frac{1}{12}$

2) The average of 6 numbers is 12. The average of 4 of those numbers is 10. What is the average of the other two numbers?

   A. 10

   B. 12

   C. 14

   D. 16

3) What is the missing term in the given sequence?

2, 3, 5, 8, 12, 17, 23, ___, 38

Write your answer in the box below.

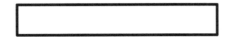

4) The average of 13, 15, 20 and x is 18. What is the value of x?

Write your answer in the box below.

5) How many possible outfit combinations come from six shirts, three slacks, and five ties?

Write your answer in the box below.

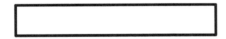

6) What is the median of these numbers? 4, 9, 13, 8, 15, 18, 5
   A. 8
   B. 9
   C. 13
   D. 15

7) A bag contains 18 balls: two green, three black, ten blue, a brown, a red and one white. If 17 balls are removed from the bag at random, what is the probability that a brown ball has NOT been removed?

A. $\dfrac{1}{9}$

B. $\dfrac{1}{6}$

C. $\dfrac{1}{18}$

D. $\dfrac{17}{18}$

8) A card is drawn at random from a standard 52–card deck, what is the probability that the card is of Hearts? (The deck includes 13 of each suit clubs, diamonds, hearts, and spades)

A. $\dfrac{1}{3}$

B. $\dfrac{1}{4}$

C. $\dfrac{1}{6}$

D. $\dfrac{1}{52}$

9) The mean of 50 test scores was calculated as 88. But, it turned out that one of the scores was misread as 94 but it was 69. What is the mean?

A. 85

B. 87

C. 87.5

D. 88.5

10) Two dice are thrown simultaneously, what is the probability of getting a sum of 6 or 9?

A. $\frac{1}{3}$

B. $\frac{1}{4}$

C. $\frac{1}{6}$

D. $\frac{1}{12}$

11) Mr. Carlos family are choosing a menu for their reception. They have 3 choices of appetizers, 5 choices of entrees, 4 choices of cake. How many different menu combinations are possible for them to choose?

A. 12

B. 32

C. 60

D. 120

12) What is the median of these numbers? 2, 27, 28, 19, 67, 44, 35

   A. 19
   B. 28
   C. 44
   D. 35

13) The average of five numbers is 24. If a sixth number 42 is added, then, what is the new average?

   A. 25
   B. 26
   C. 27
   D. 28

Answers of Worksheets – Chapter 13

Mean, Median, Mode, and Range of the Given Data

1) mean: 3, median: 2, mode: 1, 2, range: 6
2) mean: 3.625, median: 3, mode: 2, range: 5
3) mean: 5.22, median: 4, mode: 4, range: 8
4) mean: 4, median: 4, mode: 4, range: 6
5) mean: 7, median: 7, mode: 5, 7, 8, range: 4
6) mean: 4.2, median: 4, mode: 1,2,4,5,9, range: 8
7) mean: 5, median: 5, mode: 5, range: 8
8) mean: 5.78, median: 6, mode: 7, range: 7
9) mean: 5, median: 5, mode: 2, 4, 5, 6, range: 7
10) mean: 6.125, median: 5, mode: 5, range: 8
11) mean: 3, median: 2, mode: 2, 5, range: 4
12) mean: 5, median: 5, mode: none, range: 7

First Quartile, Second Quartile and Third Quartile of the Given Data

1) First quartile: 12.5, second quartile: 35, third quartile: 59.5
2) First quartile: 20, second quartile: 43.5, third quartile: 64
3) First quartile: 44.5, second quartile: 60.5, third quartile: 78.5
4) First quartile: 29, second quartile: 43, third quartile: 52
5) First quartile: 11.5, second quartile: 20.5, third quartile: 25.5
6) First quartile: 27.5, second quartile: 60, third quartile: 82.5

Box and Whisker Plots

11, 17, 22, 18, 23, 2, 3, 16, 21, 7, 8, 15, 5

Maximum: 23, Minimum: 2, Q_1: 2, Q_2: 12.5, Q_3: 19.5

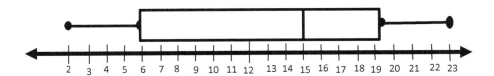

Bar Graph

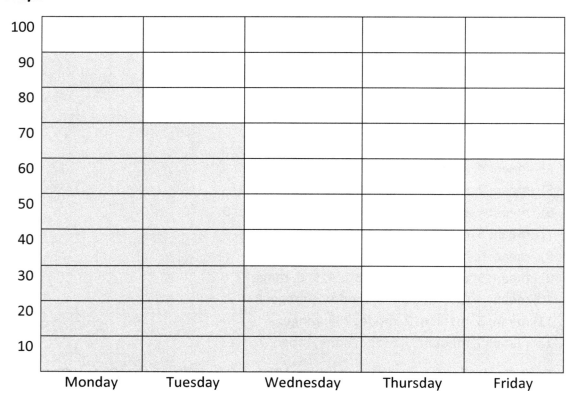

Stem–And–Leaf Plot

1)

Stem	leaf
7	2 4 9 9
8	3 6 8
9	1 5 7

2)

Stem	leaf
1	9
2	6 6 6
3	3 7
4	8 8 9

3)

Stem	leaf
4	1 2
5	3 4 4 8
6	5 5 7 9

The Pie Graph or Circle Graph

1) red
2) 15%
3) black
4) 23%
5) 13%

Scatter Plots

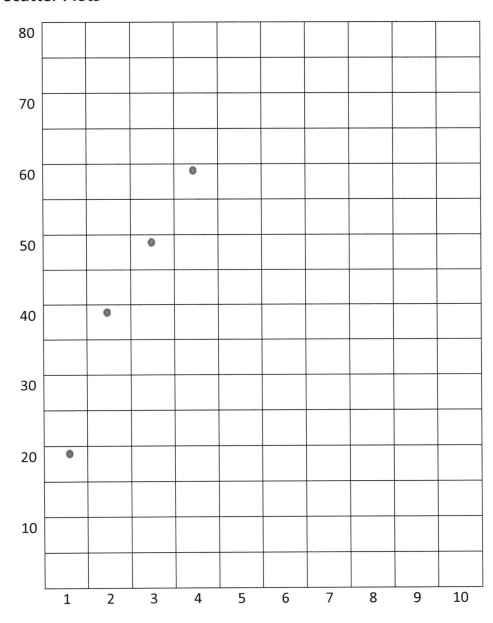

Probability of simple events

1) $\frac{2}{5}$

2) $\frac{1}{10}$

3) $\frac{1}{5}$

4) $\frac{3}{10}$

5) $\frac{3}{10}$

6) $\frac{2}{5}$

Test Preparation Answers

1) Choice B is correct.

Probability = $\frac{\text{number of desired outcomes}}{\text{number of total outcomes}} = \frac{18}{12+18+18+24} = \frac{18}{72} = \frac{1}{4}$

2) Choice D is correct

average = $\frac{\text{sum of terms}}{\text{number of terms}}$ ⇒ (average of 6 numbers) 12 = $\frac{\text{sum of numbers}}{6}$ ⇒ sum of 6 numbers is

12 × 6 = 72

(average of 4 numbers) 10 = $\frac{\text{sum of numbers}}{4}$ ⇒ sum of 4 numbers is 10 × 4 = 40

sum of 6 numbers − sum of 4 numbers = sum of 2 numbers

72 − 40 = 32

average of 2 numbers = $\frac{32}{2}$ = 16

3) The answer is 30.

Find the difference of each pairs of numbers:

2, 3, 5, 8, 12, 17, 23, ___, 38

The difference of 2 and 3 is 1, 3 and 5 is 2, 5 and 8 is 3, 8 and 12 is 4, 12 and 17 is 5, 17 and 23 is 6, 23 and next number should be 7. The number is 23 + 7 = 30

4) The answer is 24.

average = $\frac{\text{sum of terms}}{\text{number of terms}}$ ⇒ (average of 4 numbers) 18 = $\frac{\text{sum of numbers}}{4}$ ⇒ sum of 4 numbers is : $13 + 15 + 20 + x$

72 = sum of numbers ⇒ $72 = 13 + 15 + 20 + x$ ⇒ $x = 24$

5) The answer is 90.

To find the number of possible outfit combinations, multiply number of options for each factor:

$6 \times 3 \times 5 = 90$

6) Choice B is correct

Write the numbers in order:

4, 5, 8, 9, 13, 15, 18

Since we have 7 numbers (7 is odd), then the median is the number in the middle, which is 9.

7) Choice D is correct.

If 17 balls are removed from the bag at random, there will be one ball in the bag.

The probability of choosing a brown ball is 1 out of 18. Therefore, the probability of not choosing a brown ball is 17 out of 18 and the probability of having not a brown ball after removing 17 balls is the same.

8) Choice B is correct

The probability of choosing a Hearts is $13/52 = ¼$

9) Choice C is correct

average (mean) = $\frac{\text{sum of terms}}{\text{number of terms}} \Rightarrow 88 = \frac{\text{sum of terms}}{50} \Rightarrow$ sum = 88 × 50 = 4400

The difference of 94 and 69 is 25. Therefore, 25 should be subtracted from the sum.

4400 − 25 = 4375

mean = $\frac{\text{sum of terms}}{\text{number of terms}} \Rightarrow$ mean = $\frac{4375}{50}$ = 87.5

10) Choice D is correct

For Sum 6: (0 & 6) and (6 & 0), (1 & 5) and (5 & 1), (2 & 4) and (4 & 2), (3 & 3), so we have 7 options

For sum 9: (3 & 6) and (6 & 3), (4 & 5) and (5 & 14), we have 4 options.

To get a sum of 6 or 9 for two dice: 7+4=11

Since, we have 6 × 6 = 36 total options, the probability of getting a sum of 6 and 9 is 11 out of 36 or $\frac{11}{36}$.

11) Choice C is correct.

To find the number of possible outfit combinations, multiply number of options for each factor:

1 × 5 × 4 = 60

12) Choice B is correct

Write the numbers in order:

2, 19, 27, 28, 35, 44, 67

Median is the number in the middle. So, the median is 28.

13) Choice C is correct

Solve for the sum of five numbers.

average = $\dfrac{\text{sum of terms}}{\text{number of terms}} \Rightarrow 24 = \dfrac{\text{sum of 5 numbers}}{5} \Rightarrow$ sum of 5 numbers = $24 \times 5 = 120$

The sum of 5 numbers is 120. If a sixth number 42 is added, then the sum of 6 numbers is

$120 + 42 = 162$

average = $\dfrac{\text{sum of terms}}{\text{number of terms}} = \dfrac{162}{6} = 27$

PSSA Mathematics Practice Tests

Time to Test

Time to refine your skill with a practice examination

Take two practice Grade 6 PSSA Math Tests to simulate the test day experience. After you've finished, score your test using the answer key.

Before You Start

- You'll need a pencil and scratch papers to take the test.
- It's okay to guess. You won't lose any points if you're wrong.
- After you've finished the test, review the answer key to see where you went wrong.

Calculators are not permitted for PSSA Tests

PSSA Practice Test 1

The Pennsylvania System of School Assessment

Grade 6

Mathematics

2019

Grade 6 PSSA Mathematics Reference Sheet

Formulas that you may need to work questions on this test are found below. You may refer back to this page at any time during the mathematics test.

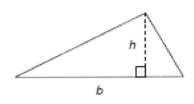

Triangle

$A = \frac{1}{2} bh$

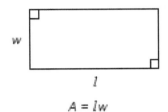

Rectangle

$A = lw$

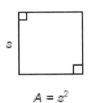

Square

$A = s^2$

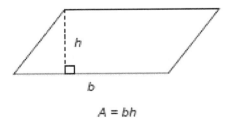

Parallelogram

$A = bh$

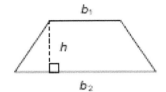

Trapezoid

$A = \frac{1}{2} h(b_1 + b_2)$

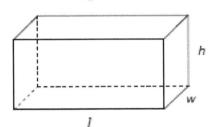

Rectangular Prism

$V = lwh \qquad SA = 2lw + 2lh + 2wh$

Cube

$V = s \cdot s \cdot s \qquad SA = 6s^2$

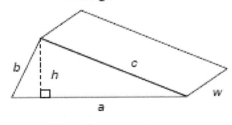

Triangular Prism

$SA = ah + aw + bw + cw$

- 20 questions
- Calculators are permitted for this practice test

1) Which expression is equivalent to $5(12x - 16)$?

   A. -20
   B. $-20x$
   C. $60x - 16$
   D. $60x - 80$

2) Which ordered pair describes point A that is shown below?

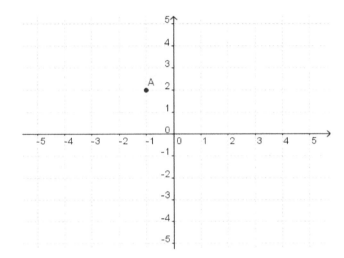

   A. $(-1, 2)$
   B. $(2, -1)$
   C. $(1, -2)$
   D. $(-2, 1)$

3) To produce a special concrete, for every 13 kg of cement, 3 liters of water is required. Which of the following ratios is the same as the ratio of cement to liters of water?

   A. 91: 21
   B. 14: 4
   C. 39: 6
   D. 9: 39

4) Find the opposite of the numbers 15, 0.

   A. $\frac{1}{15}, 0$
   B. $-15, 1$
   C. $-15, 0$
   D. $-\frac{1}{15}, 0$

5) What is the value of x in the following equation: $\quad -60 = 115 - x$

   A. 175
   B. -175
   C. 55
   D. -55

6) Which of the following graphs represents the following inequality?

$$-8 \leq 5x - 8 \leq 2$$

A.

B.

C.

D.

7) The ratio of boys to girls in a school is 4:5. If there are 765 students in the school, how many boys are in the school?

A. 612

B. 510

C. 425

D. 340

8) Martin earns $20 an hour. Which of the following inequalities represents the amount of time Martin needs to work per day to earn at least $100 per day?

   A. $20t \geq 100$
   B. $20t \leq 100$
   C. $20 + t \geq 100$
   D. $20 + t \leq 100$

9) $(55 + 5) \div 12$ is equivalent to ...

   A. $60 \div 3.4$
   B. $\frac{55}{12} + 5$
   C. $(2 \times 2 \times 3 \times 5) \div (3 \times 4)$
   D. $(2 \times 2 \times 3 \times 5) \div 3 + 4$

10) What is the value of the expression $6(2x - 3y) + (3 - 2x)^2$, when $x = 2$ and $y = -1$?

   A. -23
   B. 41
   C. 43
   D. 49

11) Round $\frac{215}{7}$ to the nearest tenth.

A. 31
B. 30.8
C. 30.7
D. 30

12) A chemical solution contains 6% alcohol. If there is 45 ml of alcohol, what is the volume of the solution?

A. 270 ml
B. 420 ml
C. 750 ml
D. 1,200 ml

13) What is the equation of a line that passes through points (0, 4) and (2, 8)?

A. $y = x$
B. $y = x + 4$
C. $y = 2x + 4$
D. $y = 2x - 4$

14) What is the volume of a box with the following dimensions?

Height = 6 cm   Width = 7 cm   Length = 9 cm

A. 63 cm³

B. 126 cm³

C. 189 cm³

D. 378 cm³

15) Anita's trick–or–treat bag contains 14 pieces of chocolate, 15 suckers, 16 pieces of gum, 20 pieces of licorice. If she randomly pulls a piece of candy from her bag, what is the probability of her pulling out a piece of sucker?

A. $\frac{1}{13}$

B. $\frac{3}{13}$

C. $\frac{14}{65}$

D. $\frac{16}{65}$

16) In the following rectangle, which statement is false?

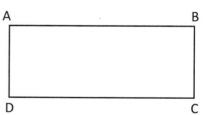

A. AD is parallel to BC

B. The measure of the sum of all the angles equals 360°.

C. Length of AB equal to length DC.

D. AB is perpendicular to AC.

17) The area of a rectangular yard is 90 square meters. What is its width if its length is 15 meters?

  A. 10 meters
  B. 8 meters
  C. 6 meters
  D. 4 meters

18) Which statement about 4 multiplied by $\frac{3}{5}$ must be true?

  A. The product is between 1 and 2
  B. The product is greater than 3
  C. The product is equal to $\frac{75}{31}$
  D. The product is between 2 and 2.5

19) Which of the following lists shows the fractions in order from least to greatest?

$$\frac{3}{4}, \frac{2}{7}, \frac{3}{8}, \frac{5}{11}$$

  A. $\frac{3}{8}, \frac{2}{7}, \frac{3}{4}, \frac{5}{11}$
  B. $\frac{2}{7}, \frac{5}{11}, \frac{3}{8}, \frac{3}{4}$
  C. $\frac{2}{7}, \frac{3}{8}, \frac{5}{11}, \frac{3}{4}$
  D. $\frac{3}{8}, \frac{2}{7}, \frac{5}{11}, \frac{3}{4}$

20) A car costing $300 is discounted 10%. Which of the following expressions can be used to find the selling price of the car?

A. $(300)(0.4)$
B. $300 - (300 \times 0.1)$
C. $(300)(0.1)$
D. $300 - (300 \times 0.9)$

This is the end of Practice Test 1

PSSA Practice Test 2

The Pennsylvania System of School Assessment

Grade 6

Mathematics

2019

Grade 6 FSA Mathematics Reference Sheet

Formulas that you may need to work questions on this test are found below. You may refer back to this page at any time during the mathematics test.

Triangle

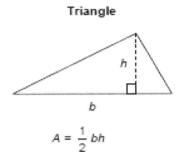

$A = \frac{1}{2} bh$

Rectangle

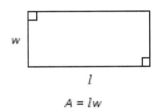

$A = lw$

Square

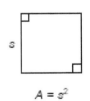

$A = s^2$

Parallelogram

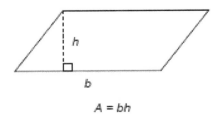

$A = bh$

Trapezoid

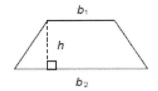

$A = \frac{1}{2} h(b_1 + b_2)$

Rectangular Prism

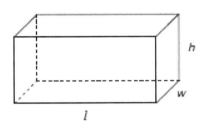

$V = lwh \qquad SA = 2lw + 2lh + 2wh$

Cube

$V = s \cdot s \cdot s \qquad SA = 6s^2$

Triangular Prism

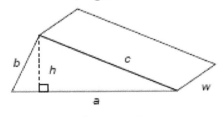

$SA = ah + aw + bw + cw$

- **20 questions**
- **Calculators are permitted for this practice test**

1) $4(1.052) - 3.126 = \cdots ?$

   A. 0.926
   B. 1.082
   C. 1.122
   D. 1.134

2) Which list shows the integer numbers listed in order from least to greatest?

   A. $-12, -4, -1, -2, 1, 3, 7$
   B. $-12, -1, -2, -4, 1, 3, 7$
   C. $-12, -4, -2, -1, 1, 3, 7$
   D. $-1, -2, -4, -12, 1, 3, 7$

3) There are 55 blue marbles and 143 red marbles. We want to place these marbles in some boxes so that there is the same number of red marbles in each box and the same number of blue marbles in each of the boxes. How many boxes do we need?

   A. 8
   B. 9
   C. 10
   D. 11

4) What is the value of the following expression?

$$2{,}205 \div 315$$

A. 5
B. 6
C. 7
D. 8

5) Solve the following equation.

$$112 = 22 + x$$

A. $x = -90$
B. $x = 90$
C. $x = -134$
D. $x = 134$

6) Car A travels 221.5 km at a given time, while car B travels 1.2 times the distance car A travels at the same time. What is the distance car B travels during that time?

A. 222.7 km
B. 233.5 km
C. 241.5 km
D. 265.8 km

7) The perimeter of the trapezoid below is 38. What is its area?

A. 198 cm²
B. 162 cm²
C. 99 cm²
D. 81 cm²

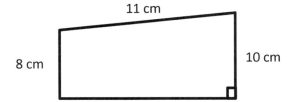

8) Which of the following expressions has the greatest value?

A. $3^1 + 12$
B. $3^3 - 3^2$
C. $3^4 - 60$
D. $3^5 - 218$

9) The diameter of a circle is π. What is the area of the circle?

A. $2\pi^2$
B. π^2
C. $\dfrac{\pi^3}{3}$
D. $\dfrac{\pi^3}{4}$

10) Alfred has x apples. Alvin has 40 apples, which is 15 apples less than number of apples Alfred owns. If Baron has $\frac{1}{5}$ times as many apples as Alfred has. How many apples does Baron have?

A. 5
B. 11
C. 55
D. 275

11) In the following triangle find α.

A. 100°
B. 90°
C. 60°
D. 30°

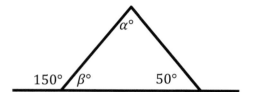

12) The price of a laptop is decreased by 15% to $425. What is its original price?

A. $283
B. $430
C. $500
D. $550

13) Find the perimeter of shape in the following figure? (all angles are right angles)

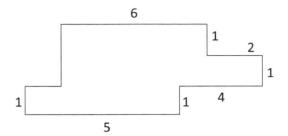

A. 21

B. 22

C. 24

D. 20

14) What is the probability of choosing a month starts with A in a year?

A. 1

B. $\frac{2}{3}$

C. $\frac{1}{2}$

D. $\frac{1}{6}$

15) What are the values of mode and median in the following set of numbers?

1, 3, 3, 6, 6, 5, 4, 3, 1, 1, 2

A. Mode: 1, 2, Median: 2
B. Mode: 1, 3, Median: 3
C. Mode: 2, 3, Median: 2
D. Mode: 1, 3, Median: 2.5

16) Which expression equivalent to $x \times 92$?

   A. $(x \times 90) + 2$
   B. $x \times 9 \times 2$
   C. $(x \times 90) + (x \times 2)$
   D. $(x \times 90) + 2$

17) The ratio of pens to pencils in a box is 3 to 5. If there are 96 pens and pencils in the box altogether, how many more pens should be put in the box to make the ratio of pens to pencils 1 : 1?

   A. 22
   B. 23
   C. 24
   D. 25

18) If point A placed at $-\frac{24}{3}$ on a number line, which of the following points has a distance equal to 5 from point A?

   A. -13
   B. -3
   C. -2
   D. A and B

19) Which of the following shows the numbers in increasing order?

A. $\frac{3}{13}, \frac{4}{11}, \frac{5}{14}, \frac{2}{5}$

B. $\frac{3}{13}, \frac{5}{14}, \frac{4}{11}, \frac{2}{5}$

C. $\frac{3}{13}, \frac{5}{14}, \frac{2}{5}, \frac{4}{11}$

D. $\frac{5}{14}, \frac{3}{13}, \frac{2}{5}, \frac{4}{11}$

20) If $x = -4$, which of the following equations is true?

A. $x(3x - 1) = 50$

B. $5(11 - x^2) = -25$

C. $3(-2x + 5) = 49$

D. $x(-5x - 19) = -3$

This is the end of Practice Test 2

PSSA Math Practice Tests Answers and Explanations

PSSA Math Practice Test 1		PSSA Math Practice Test 2	
1	D	1	B
2	A	2	C
3	A	3	D
4	C	4	C
5	A	5	B
6	B	6	D
7	D	7	D
8	A	8	D
9	C	9	D
10	C	10	B
11	C	11	A
12	C	12	C
13	C	13	C
14	D	14	D
15	B	15	B
16	D	16	C
17	C	17	C
18	D	18	D
19	C	19	B
20	B	20	B

PSSA Math Practice Test 1 Answers and Explanations

1) **Choice D is correct**

   $5(12x - 16) = (5 \times 12x) - (5 \times 16) = (5 \times 12)x - (5 \times 16) = 60x - 80$

2) **Choice A is correct**

   The coordinate plane has two axes. The vertical line is called the y-axis and the horizontal is called the x-axis. The points on the coordinate plane are address using the form (x, y). The point A is one unit on the left side of x-axis, therefore its x value is -1 and it is two units up, therefore its y axis is 2. The coordinate of the point is: $(-1, 2)$

3) **Choice A is correct**

   $91 : 21 = 13 : 3$

   $13 \times 7 = 91$ And $3 \times 7 = 21$

4) **Choice C is correct**

   Opposite number of any number x is a number that if added to x, the result is 0. Then:

   $15 + (-15) = 0$ and $0 + 0 = 0$

5) **Choice A is correct**

   $-60 = 115 - x$

   First, subtract 115 from both sides of the equation. Then:

   $-60 - 115 = 115 - 115 - x \to -175 = -x$

   Multiply both sides by (-1):

   $\to x = 175$

6) **Choice B is correct**

   $-8 \leq 5x - 8 < 2 \rightarrow$ (add 8 all sides) $-8 + 8 \leq 5x - 8 + 8 < 2 + 8 \rightarrow 0 \leq 5x < 10$
   $\rightarrow$ (divide all sides by 5) $0 \leq x < 2$

7) **Choice D is correct**

   The ratio of boy to girls is 4:5. Therefore, there are 4 boys out of 9 students. To find the answer, first divide the total number of students by 9, then multiply the result by 4.

   $765 \div 9 = 85 \Rightarrow 85 \times 4 = 340$

8) **Choice A is correct**

   For one hour he earns $20, then for t hours he earns $20t$. If he wants to earn at least $100, therefor, the number of working hours multiplied by 20 must be equal to 100 or more than 100.

   $$20t \geq 100$$

9) **Choice C is correct**

   $(55 + 5) \div (12) = (60) \div (12)$

   The prime factorization of 60 is: $2 \times 2 \times 3 \times 5$

   The prime factorization of 12 is: 3×4

   Therefore: $(60) \div (12) = (2 \times 2 \times 3 \times 5) \div (3 \times 4)$

10) **Choice C is correct**

    Plug in the value of x and y and use order of operations rule.

    $x = 2$ and $y = -1$

    $6(2x - 3y) + (3 - 2x)^2 = 6(2(2) - 3(-1)) + (3 - 2(2))^2 = 6(4 + 3) + (-1)^2 = 42 + 1 = 43$

11) **Choice C is correct**

    $\dfrac{215}{7} \cong 30.71 \cong 30.7$

12) **Choice C is correct**

    6% of the volume of the solution is alcohol. Let x be the volume of the solution.

Then: 6% of x = 45 ml $\Rightarrow$ 0.06 x = 45 $\Rightarrow$ x = 45 ÷ 0.06 = 750

13) Choice C is correct

The slope of the line is: $\frac{y_2-y_1}{x_2-x_1} = \frac{8-4}{2-0} = \frac{4}{2} = 2$

The equation of a line can be written as:

$y - y_0 = m(x - x_0) \rightarrow y - 4 = 2(x - 0) \rightarrow y - 4 = 2x \rightarrow y = 2x + 4$

14) Choice D is correct

Volume of a box = length × width × height = 6 × 7 × 9 = 378

15) Choice B is correct

Probability = $\frac{number\ of\ desired\ outcomes}{number\ of\ total\ outcomes} = \frac{15}{14+15+16+20} = \frac{15}{65} = \frac{3}{13}$

16) Choice D is correct

In any rectangle, sides are not perpendicular to diagonals.

17) Choice C is correct

Let y be the width of the rectangle. Then; $15 \times y = 90 \rightarrow y = \frac{90}{15} = 6$

18) Choice D is correct

$4 \times \frac{3}{5} = \frac{12}{5} = 2.4$

A. $2.4 > 2$

B. $2.4 < 3$

C. $\frac{75}{31} = 2.419 \neq 2.4$

D. $2 < 2.4 < 2.5$ This is the answer!

19) Choice C is correct

Let's compare each fraction:

$\frac{2}{7} < \frac{3}{8} < \frac{5}{11} < \frac{3}{4}$

Only choice C provides the right order.

20) Choice B is correct

To find the discount, multiply the number $(100\% - \text{rate of discount})$

Therefore; $300(100\% - 10\%) = 300(1 - 0.1) = 300 - (300 \times 0.1)$

PSSA Math Practice Test 2 Answers and Explanations

1) **Choice B is correct**

    $4(1.052) - 3.126 = 4.208 - 3.126 = 1.082$

2) **Choice C is correct**

    $-12 < -4 < -2 < -1 < 1 < 3 < 7$

    Then choice C is correct

3) **Choice D is correct**

    First, we need to find the GCF (Greatest Common Factor) of 143 and 55.

    $143 = 11 \times 13$

    $55 = 5 \times 11 \rightarrow$ GFC = 11

    Therefore, we need 11 boxes.

4) **Choice C is correct**

    $2205 \div 315 = \dfrac{2205}{315} = \dfrac{441}{63} = \dfrac{147}{21} = 7$

5) **Choice B is correct**

    $112 = 22 + x$

    Subtract 22 from both sides of the equation. Then:

    $x = 112 - 22 = 90$

6) **Choice D is correct**

    Distance that car B travels $= 1.2 \times$ distance that car A travels

    $= 1.2 \times 221.5 = 265.8$ Km

7) Choice D is correct

The perimeter of the trapezoid is 38.

Therefore, the missing side (height) is $= 38 - 8 - 10 - 11 = 9$

Area of the trapezoid: $A = \frac{1}{2} h (b1 + b2) = \frac{1}{2} (9) (8 + 10) = 81$

8) Choice D is correct

A. $3^1 + 12 = 3 + 12 = 15$

B. $3^3 - 3^2 = 27 - 9 = 18$

C. $3^4 - 60 = 81 - 60 = 21$

D. $3^5 - 218 = 243 - 218 = 25$

9) Choice D is correct

The radius of the circle is: $\frac{\pi}{2}$

The area of circle: $\pi r^2 = \pi (\frac{\pi}{2})^2 = \pi \times \frac{\pi^2}{4} = \frac{\pi^3}{4}$

10) Choice B is correct

Alfred has x apple which is 15 apples more than number of apples Alvin owns. Therefore:

$x - 15 = 40 \rightarrow x = 40 + 15 = 55$

Alfred has 55 apples.

Let y be the number of apples that Baron has. Then: $y = \frac{1}{5} \times 55 = 11$

11) Choice A is correct

Complementary angles add up to 180 degrees.

$\beta + 150° = 180° \rightarrow \beta = 180° - 150° = 30°$

The sum of all angles in a triangle is 180 degrees. Then:

$\alpha + \beta + 50° = 180° \rightarrow \alpha + 30° + 50° = 180°$

$\rightarrow \alpha + 80° = 180° \rightarrow \alpha = 180° - 80° = 100°$

12) Choice C is correct

Let x be the original price.

If the price of a laptop is decreased by 15% to $425, then: $85\% \text{ of } x = 425 \Rightarrow 0.85x = 425$

$\Rightarrow x = 425 \div 0.85 = 500$

13) Choice C is correct

Let x and y be two sides of the shape. Then:

$x + 1 = 1 + 1 + 1 \rightarrow x = 2$

$y + 6 + 2 = 5 + 4 \rightarrow y + 8 = 9 \rightarrow y = 1$

Then, the perimeter is:

$1 + 5 + 1 + 4 + 1 + 2 + 1 + 6 + 2 + 1 = 24$

14) Choice D is correct

Two months, April and August, in 12 months start with A, then:

Probability = $\dfrac{\text{number of desired outcomes}}{\text{number of total outcomes}} = \dfrac{2}{12} = \dfrac{1}{6}$

15) Choice B is correct

First, put the numbers in order from least to greatest: 1, 1, 1, 2, 3, 3, 3, 4, 5, 6, 6

The Mode of the set of numbers is: 1 and 3 (the most frequent numbers)

Median is: 3 (the number in the middle)

16) Choice C is correct

$x \times 92 = x \times (90 + 2) = (x \times 90) + (x \times 2)$

17) Choice C is correct

The ratio of pens to pencils is 3 : 5. Therefore there are 3 pens out of all 8 pens and pencils. To find the answer, first dived 96 by 8 then multiply the result by 3.

$96 \div 8 = 12 \rightarrow 12 \times 3 = 36$

There are 36 pens and 60 pencils (96-36). Therefore, 24 more pens should be put in the box to make the ratio 1 : 1

18) Choice D is correct

If the value of point A is greater than the value of point B, then the distance of two points on the number line is: value of A− value of B

A. $-\frac{24}{3} - (-13) = -8 + 13 = 5 = 5$

B. $-3 - \left(-\frac{24}{3}\right) = -3 + 8 = 5 = 5$

C. $-2 - \left(-\frac{24}{3}\right) = -2 + 8 = 6 \neq 5$

19) **Choice B is correct**

$\frac{3}{13} \cong 0.23 \qquad \frac{5}{14} \cong 0.357 \qquad \frac{4}{11} \cong 0.36 \qquad \frac{2}{5} = 0.4$

Then:

$$\frac{3}{13} < \frac{5}{14} < \frac{4}{11} < \frac{2}{5}$$

20) **Choice B is correct**

Plugin the value of x in the equations. $x = -4$, then:

E. $x(3x - 1) = 50 \rightarrow -4(3(-4) - 1) = -4(-12 - 1) = -4(-13) = 52 \neq 50$

$5(11 - x^2) = -25 \rightarrow 5(11 - (-4)^2) = 5(11 - 16) = 5(-5) = -25$

F. $3(-2x + 5) = 49 \rightarrow 3(-2(-4) + 5) = 3(8 + 5) = 39 \neq 49$

G. $x(-5x - 19) = -3 \rightarrow -4(-5(-4) - 19 = -4(20 - 19) = -4 \neq -3$

$5(11 - (-4)^2) = 5(11 - 16) = 5(-5) = -25$

"Effortless Math Education" Publications

Effortless Math authors' team strives to prepare and publish the best quality Mathematics learning resources to make learning Math easier for all. We hope that our publications help you or your student learn Math in an effective way.

We all in Effortless Math wish you good luck and successful studies!

Effortless Math Authors

Online Math Lessons

Enjoy interactive Math lessons online

with the best Math teachers

Online Math learning that's effective, affordable, flexible, and fun

Learn Math wherever you want; when you want
Ultimate flexibility. You can now learn Math online, enjoy high quality engaging lessons no matter where in the world you are. It's affordable too.

Learn Math with one-on-one classes
We provide one-on-one Math tutoring online. We believe that one-to-one tutoring is the most effective way to learn Math.

Qualified Math tutors
Working with the best Math tutors in the world is the key to success! Our tutors give you the support and motivation you need to succeed with a personal touch.

Online Math Lessons

It's easy! Here's how it works.

1- Request a FREE introductory session.

2- Meet a Math tutor online.

3- Start Learning Math in Minutes.

Send Email to: info@EffortlessMath.com

CPSIA information can be obtained
at www.ICGtesting.com
Printed in the USA
BVHW010809181218
535793BV00017B/283/P